SURVIVOR

One Man's Victory Over Cancer

GREG CARTER

SURVIVOR: ONE MAN'S VICTORY OVER CANCER by Greg Carter
Published by Creation House Press
A part of Strang Communications Company
600 Rinehart Road
Lake Mary, Florida 32746
www.creationhouse.com

Scripture quotations marked AMP are from the Amplified Bible. Old Testament copyright © 1965, 1987 by the Zondervan Corporation. The Amplified New Testament copyright © 1954, 1958, 1987 by the Lockman Foundation. Used by permission.

Scripture quotations marked KJV are from the King James Version of the Bible.

Scripture quotations marked NKJV are from the New King James Version of the Bible. Copyright © 1979, 1980, 1982 by Thomas Nelson, Inc., publishers. Used by permission.

Scripture quotations marked NIV are from the Holy Bible, New International Version. Copyright © 1973, 1978, 1984, International Bible Society. Used by permission.

Scripture quotations marked NCV are from The Holy Bible, New Century Version. Copyright © 1987, 1988, 1991 by Word Publishing, Dallas, Texas 75039. Used by permission.

Cover design by Terry Clifton
Interior design by David Bilby

Library of Congress Control Number: 2003102645
International Standard Book Number: 1-59185-194-7

Printed in the United States of America.
03 04 05 06 07   8 7 6 5 4 3 2 1

To contact the author for personal encouragement or to schedule a service:
Greg Carter
8620 South Harrison Park Road
Laconia, IN 47135
812-969-3223
Larev@msn.com

CONTENTS

ACKNOWLEDGMENTS

Let me take a moment to acknowledge those who helped me overcome:

My wife, Ronda, who not only shared this journey with me but became a tremendous source of stability along the way.

My parents, Ned and Bonnie Carter, who were a constant source of encouragement.

Nurse Marcia Brown, my sister, whose numerous phone calls lifted my spirits and answered all my medical questions.

The church at Grace Tabernacle, where I have pastored for the past twenty-three years, who loved me more than themselves and stood in the gap for me when I was too weak to fight.

Kevin Helton and Sandi Pike for their technical expertise and help in making this project a reality.

My cousins Art La Duke, who lost his battle with cancer, and Steve La Duke for their financial assistance in bringing this book to life.

Rodney Howard-Browne for being such a gracious host in New Orleans, St. Louis and Tampa and praying for us morning, noon and night during those meetings.

FOREWORD

"You have cancer!" These words strike fear in the hearts of hundreds of people every day. In many cases, cancer is a death sentence, and when the diagnosis is made, you feel as if you are suddenly and unexpectedly being sentenced to death row for something you never did. When a person has cancer, even though they are alive, death begins to take over their bodies. This is the story of a man who fought back from the brink of death all the way to a clean bill of health by the power of the word of God.

Pastor Greg Carter was diagnosed with bladder cancer in 1995. I have known Pastor Greg and his wife, Ronda, for fourteen years. Theirs was the first church in which I had the privilege of ministering on my first ministry trip to the United States in 1987. At that time, the town of Laconia, Indiana, had a population of sixty-five, but the Carter's church overflowed with people during my last crusade there. Their church is a lighthouse to the entire community. Pastors Greg and Ronda have been faithfully serving God all these years in Laconia, and it was a shock to hear that he had been diagnosed with cancer.

Even though the word *cancer* strikes fear in the hearts of most people, Greg was determined not to give up—to just lie down and die—but to fight it. During the dark times, he came and joined us in several of our revival meetings that we were conducting all over the nation. We would pray with him, lay our hands on him, and trust God with him for his miracle. We felt that God would touch his body if we could just get him saturated under the anointing of the Holy Spirit.

We need each other. We need to stand with our heavenly family. We are the body of Christ. We need to be strong for our brothers and sisters when they are under attack. We need to pray for each other and join our faith together with theirs. We need to press in with them for their miracle.

Pastor Greg put his trust in God and His word, and he has come through victoriously. Thanks to the power of God, now five years later, he has a clean bill of health. Once again, we can rejoice in the fact that God is faithful! Even cancer must bow its knee to the King of kings and the Lord of lords!

I believe that this book will be a great blessing and an inspiration to you.

DR. RODNEY M. HOWARD-BROWNE
TAMPA, FLORIDA

You Need to Hear a Survivor's Story

T HIS IS NOT a "how to" book giving you ten easy steps to conquer cancer. It is not a testimony of how great faith and persistence in prayer eventually saved the day. It is simply the story of an eighteen-month chapter of my life that cancer indelibly impacted. Every chapter since has been influenced by my encounter with this life-altering disease.

In January 1996, because of bladder cancer and massive lymph node involvement, doctors at the IUPUI hospital in Indianapolis gave me less than a year to live. This book details my journey through the most difficult days of my life. It is a survivor's story proclaiming the great mercy and faithfulness of the God we serve. It is the story of human frailty being strengthened daily by an infusion of divine life. It is the story of battle after battle culminating in eventual victory.

In the following pages, I want to encourage those who are going through a devastating time in their journey through life. All the answers to your questions are not here, but hopefully, there will be enough realism to allow you to understand that there are those who have already won the fight you are now waging. I have tried to share honestly my ups and downs, my highs and lows, and my times of great faith as well as utter despair. I lost a few battles but eventually won the war.

When I was struggling to keep afloat, I often read accounts of those who had survived cancer. Those who have engaged in a battle for their lives and lived to tell about it have much to say to those who are presently in the fight.

Those resources became a source of sustenance for me that gave me the strength to endure another day. During my darkest days I often promised myself that one day I would write a book that would do for others what their testimonies had done for me.

Sometimes you need to hear a survivor's story. It is my prayer that this book will be a lifeline thrown out to anyone perishing in a sea of turmoil. May God Almighty encourage you in His grace as you read this book.

CHAPTER 1

All Is Well,
Then Suddenly…

L IFE IS WHAT happens while we are making other plans. Not realizing that devastating events were lurking just around the corner, my future, with all my carefully laid plans, was about to be drastically altered. The Holy Scriptures tell us to take no thought for tomorrow because "each day has enough trouble of its own" (Matthew 6:34, NCV). But even as a minister full of life, trying to live in the flow of God, I, like so many others, lived my life with all sorts of future plans, thinking that nothing would stop their fulfillment.

Several months before a scheduled mission trip to India, Steve Rayborn, one of my closest friends, and his wife, Cindy, were vacationing with Ronda and me in the Smokies in August of 1995. Steve and I love to play golf, while our wives love to hit the outlet malls.

As I hit my tee shot on the first hole, I felt a twinge of pain that was unlike anything I had ever felt before. It was not severe, just strange; I could not determine its source. It left as mysteriously as it came, and I felt no more sensations of pain on the front nine. Later, I noticed blood in my urine. I was no medical expert, but I knew that I needed to get it checked out as soon as possible.

Not wanting to ruin Ronda's vacation, I determined to tell her nothing. We would enjoy our week together, and I would make an appointment with an urologist as soon as we got home. *Whatever is wrong must be something simple, like an infection or non-malignant growth that will be easily treatable,* I reassured myself each time I passed blood. *I'll see a doctor, get some antibiotics, get over this thing and go on with my life.*

When we arrived home from vacation, I broke the news to Ronda and made an appointment with Dr. Joseph Bruckman at Southern Indiana Urology for the last Tuesday in August. After an examination and urine analysis, Dr. Bruckman very compassionately informed me that there were cancer cells in my urine, and he needed to examine inside my urinary tract with a cystoscope. He scheduled the procedure for the following Monday.

Early Monday morning Ronda and I arrived at Floyd Memorial Hospital in New Albany, Indiana, and I was admitted as an outpatient. Dr. Bruckman performed a procedure inserting a cystoscope device into my urinary tract while I was under anesthesia. After completing the procedure, Dr. Bruckman signed release papers and scheduled an appointment on Thursday to discuss the results of the test. Ronda and I went home that afternoon fully assured that the results would be something simple, treatable, and well within our limits to handle.

During the Wednesday evening service, many dear church friends prayed passionately for Ronda and me. We had a wonderful service and, despite the next day's visit to the doctor, I felt a remarkable peace about my circumstances. Little did I know that in just a few short hours that peace would be shattered, and I would be embarking on a journey through the deepest wilderness I had ever known.

All Is Well, Then Suddenly...

SOME KIND OF A BAD DREAM

Thursday, after arriving at Dr. Bruckman's office and going through the routine preliminaries, I settled down in a soft chair and waited for my name to be called, playing over and over in my mind all the possibilities of different diagnoses.

When my name was called, I took Ronda's hand and walked back through the corridor to the doctor's office. A nurse seated us and told us that the doctor would see us momentarily.

As Dr. Bruckman entered and sat across from us at his desk, I saw a look of deep concern and impending bad news in his countenance. Instead of any formalities of greeting, he simply began to read the biopsy report and his diagnosis, based on the pathologist's findings.

His news: I had two malignant tumors—Grade III Transitional Cell Carcinoma—that had penetrated the wall of my bladder. The invasive cancer had penetrated so deeply that removing it through a cystoscope was not possible.

A radical cystectomy, a surgical procedure that involves removal of the bladder and the prostate gland, was the doctor's advised treatment. A urinary diversion known as an ileal loop would take the place of my cancerous bladder. A section of my colon would be used internally to direct the urine flow to an ostomy, or hole in my side that would drain into an appliance, literally a plastic bag attached to my abdomen. This device would require draining every few hours. I was assured that despite this inconvenience, I could return to a normal life.

"Today is Thursday, and I would like to operate on Monday," were the words I heard the doctor say, but they sounded as if they were coming from some distant place.

Both Ronda and I were completely stunned by the diagnosis. Never did we believe that anything of this magnitude

11

could happen to me. I was a pastor, full of faith, preaching the gospel, and praying for the sick at almost every church service. *This had to be some kind of bad dream.*

Mustering all the strength and courage I could, I asked Dr. Bruckman, "What if I choose to do nothing?"

He responded simply, "If you do not have your bladder removed, the cancer will penetrate through your bladder wall, spread to other areas, and you will die. Your only hope of long term survival is to have surgery."

After hearing this devastating news, I was in no shape to make any immediate decision about surgery. I asked for the weekend to think over the matter and pray for God's direction before I made any decision. Dr. Bruckman graciously consented, shook my hand, and scheduled an appointment for the following Monday.

The ride home was uncharacteristically quiet. Ronda and I could not even put into words the utter despair and helplessness we both felt. She drove, weeping quietly as I stared at the familiar scenery along Highway 11, trying desperately to put a positive spin on my circumstances.

Sleep that night evaded us. Weeping softly, Ronda lay next to me while I battled spirits of fear and self-pity. I had handled some difficult situations before, but nothing like this. Doubts about the integrity of the God I served and my relationship to Him began gnawing at my faith. *Why has God allowed this to happen to me?* and *Is there a way out?* were questions I had at that moment with no answers.

Friday morning, I became aware of the stark reality that it is hard to pray with faith when you are faced with a devastating medical report. I soon realized that my relationship with Jesus was going to have to expand to places that I had never been spiritually.

That evening at Grace Tabernacle's intercessory prayer service, folks who did not normally participate came in force to pray for my situation. If intensity of prayer and tears will get you healed, the cancer in my body did not stand a chance. I was amazed at the people who were standing with me, touched with the feelings of my infirmity.

WAITING UPON GOD

Late Sunday evening, I arrived at a course of action. After three days of prayer, a consultation with my sister, Marcia Brown, who is a registered nurse, and the consent of my wife, I decided to persuade Dr. Bruckman to give me some time to seek God for a healing. I understood the medical ramifications of such a decision, but I could not bring myself just to lie down and have surgery until I had given the Lord time to heal my body.

Our Monday morning consultation with the doctor went even better than I anticipated. Dr. Bruckman, a respected urologist, had always done things by the medical book, but he understood that, as a pastor, I was not going to have surgery until I had determined I had exhausted every spiritual avenue of healing.

Very reluctantly, making sure I completely understood the danger of waiting, and with my full consent, Dr. Bruckman proposed we wait ninety days. After that period of time, I would have a second biopsy and, if nothing had changed, I would consent to surgery. I left his office full of hope. *Surely*, I reasoned, *if God created the world in six days, taking care of my little problem in ninety days was nothing for Him.*

During the following three months, I engaged in some of the most intense times of spiritual warfare I had ever known. Daily, I prayed with intense fervor, seeking God's healing touch. I quoted the Word to myself to build my faith, submitted myself to all who wanted to pray for me, and underwent a personal inspection of my spiritual life to remove any defilement that might block a touch of God. I went on several retreats to isolated places in order to spend large amounts of undisturbed time seeking God. My parents, Ned and Bonnie Carter, accompanied Ronda and me to Brownsville Assembly of God in Pensacola, Florida, in hopes that God's healing power would touch me as He was touching others daily in the revival services. I did everything I could think of to stay in a spiritual atmosphere where God could find me and touch me.

Spiritual Journeys Can Have Unexpected Turns

Even though my physical symptoms were screaming otherwise, I arrived at the hospital on December fourth for my cystoscope procedure, charged with faith and confidence that the biopsy report would reveal that God had touched me and that surgery would no longer be necessary.

Cystourethroscopy usually lasts a relatively short time, and after a few hours in the recovery room and a glass of orange juice, the patient is sent home. This time I was not so fortunate. The scope had irritated my urinary tract and the opening to my bladder, making urination difficult, and it was decided that I was to be kept overnight for observation.

After a very uncomfortable night, my spiritual disposition had shifted from anticipation of a good report to horrible dread of a bad one. But as negative as my disposition was, it was about to take a nosedive.

The biopsy report not only revealed that I still had Grade III Transitional Cell Carcinoma, but it also revealed that the tumors had increased in size and had invaded deeper into the wall of my bladder. Anger swept over me like a raging river. Dr. Bruckman left the room, and I asked everyone present to leave and give me some time. When the door to my room had closed and I was completely alone, I exploded. I threw pillows, urinals, pitchers, newspapers and magazines—anything that was not nailed down.

In my confusion, I had questions that demanded answers. Why hadn't God touched me? How, after such an intense time of spiritual warfare, could the situation have grown worse? I was so angry with God for letting me down. I thought, *I could have been out robbing banks and committing adultery for the past ninety days and gotten this report.*

I sat down on the bed and looked upward, beholding only ceiling tile, and told the Lord that I would never preach another sermon, and as soon as possible, I was going to resign my church, quit the ministry, and go back to teaching school. "It's your fault!" I shouted at God. "I proclaimed to everyone who would listen that You were going to heal me, and You didn't. How can I ever stand behind a pulpit again and proclaim anything good about You when You didn't hold up Your end of the bargain?"

If there was ever an outburst that deserved a lightening bolt, that was it. But as my anger began to subside, I became fully aware that I could not become separated from God, the source of my help. I asked God's forgiveness for my outburst and direction for the decisions I would be forced to make in the coming days.

According to the medical report, if I wanted to be around much longer, I was going to have to undergo radical cystectomy, a surgical procedure that involved the removal of my bladder and prostate and would require me to wear a urostomy pouch, as well as leaving me sexually dysfunctional.

Things were certainly not following the script I had written in my mind. My well-thought-out plans were that God would heal me in that ninety-day period, we would have a celebration at church, God would get the glory, and

I would go back to business as usual. Instead, I was facing a horrific surgery, a long recuperation, and spiritual egg on my face.

THOUGHTS, PLANS AND MEDICAL OPTIONS

I determined that if I was forced to have medical intervention, I would become as informed as I could about all the possible avenues of treatment. The probability of wearing a urostomy pouch and being sexually dysfunctional at the age of forty-three was a tough thing to swallow. Thoughts that somewhere there was a doctor who had a more appealing option dominated my thinking for days.

Finally, the first ray of hope surfaced one Wednesday night before church as Paula Murphy, our dear friend, brought us some information she had gleaned from the Internet. She brought us several pages of medical reports about a procedure called neobladder. Neobladder surgery involved the construction of a continent urinary reservoir from a section of the patient's colon. A nerve-sparing procedure, in some cases, could also be performed, restoring sexual function. Of all the options for which I had information, this certainly seemed to be the one I was most attracted to, and the medical center where the procedure was performed was only one hundred twenty-five miles from my home.

At our next consultation with Dr. Bruckman, I expressed my desire not to have the ileal loop procedure and wanted to check into the neobladder. He graciously agreed to contact Dr. Randall Rowland at the IUPUI Medical Center in Indianapolis, Indiana—one of the few places where this procedure is done.

After Dr. Bruckman's call, Dr. Rowland, head of Urology at IUPUI, agreed to meet with me and discuss the possibility of surgery. Although nowhere near elation,

I was slowly coming to grips with the reality that I was going to have to make the best of a bad situation.

Ronda and I found Dr. Rowland, a world-renowned surgeon, to be very kind and compassionate. After reviewing Dr. Bruckman's findings and going over the results of the most recent CT scan, Dr. Rowland agreed to take my case and scheduled me for surgery three weeks later. I took a degree of comfort in his knowledge and experience. His vast medical expertise included over three hundred of these procedures. If I had to have this surgery, this gentleman was certainly the man I wanted doing it.

Urination was becoming increasingly more difficult and frequent. I also felt like a spiritual failure to a degree because my faith could not overcome this illness that was waging war in my physical body. To make matters worse, I felt shunned by some of my Christian friends because I had agreed to surgery; to them, I was not taking a stand of faith.

I knew in my spirit that the next three weeks would be a wild roller-coaster ride of emotions, accentuated by both highs and lows. My hope was that I could ride this thing out while I continued to minister to the needs of my congregation.

God always has a way of escape (see 1 Corinthians 10:13), no matter how difficult the trial, and that escape is usually spiritual growth. The fiery ordeals that all of us will encounter at some time in life will either make us or break us. If we determine to pass through whatever spiritual wilderness we find ourselves in, it will require us to develop spiritual strength we did not possess when we began the journey. In the middle of the trek, we run out of vitality, and if we are to survive, we must allow the Holy Spirit to develop within us spiritual resources that were there all along, just unknown to us.

ENCOURAGEMENT KNOWS NO DISTANCE

Encouragement came to me from a phone call from Rodney Howard-Browne, a well-known evangelist from South Africa. When Rodney arrived in the United States in 1987, the first church he ministered in was the church I pastor, Grace Tabernacle in Laconia, Indiana. During that time, I was hosting a weekly television program, *Still in the Spirit,* and Rodney did a month-long series of programs with me sharing his vision for America.

Over the next few years, Rodney conducted several revival meetings in our church, and we developed a bond of friendship. After his last visit to our church in 1991, I had little contact with Rodney because the scope of his international ministry had broadened well beyond the little town of Laconia, and I was thrilled that God was using him so mightily.

My fifteen-year-old son, Dane, desperately wanting to see me healed, called Rodney and asked him to pray for me. Rodney, however, did more than just pray. At his expense, the week before my surgery, he invited Ronda and me to attend his Winter Camp Meeting in Tampa. Hotel accommodations, meals and transportation, as well as spiritual refreshing, were waiting for us as we landed at the Tampa International Airport.

Bad weather conditions had delayed our flight out of Louisville, Kentucky, causing us to miss the Monday morning service and part of the evening service. A representative of Rodney's ministry met us at the airport and whisked us to the Tampa Sun Dome where thousands of hungry believers from all parts of the globe soaked in the presence of God.

By the time we entered the building, the worship service was just coming to its conclusion. Trying to be as inconspicuous as possible, Ronda and I slipped into our seats, removed our jackets, and tried to take in one of the most spiritual atmospheres we had ever been in. Thousands of people were worshipping the Lord, and the presence of God was so thick you could cut it with a knife. *Surely,* I thought, *there is healing in this place.*

In the midst of this glorious atmosphere, I heard my name being called out. Rodney had spotted us and wanted me to come to the platform for prayer. As I walked down the aisle, Rodney told the audience who I was and why I was there. I heard him say that he was going to pray for me in every service and believe God for a miracle. Those were the last words I heard.

As Rodney stretched his hand toward me, the power of God hit me with such force that I fell to the floor. I felt as if I were plugged into an electric outlet. Rodney literally lay on top of me much like Elisha did the Shunammite widow's son, tearfully asking God to heal my body. For the next three hours, I experienced the most profound touch of God I had ever had upon my life. Wave after wave of the power of God rushed through my body causing my whole body to vibrate and tremble.

When the spiritual fog began to subside, I lifted my hands toward heaven and began to implore the Lord to heal my body. After an experience like that, I reasoned that surely the next item on the Lord's agenda would be to sweep over my body and cleanse me from sickness. Between sobs I prayed, "Heal me, Jesus. Heal me, Jesus."

The Holy Spirit spoke to me as clearly as I had ever heard Him speak in my life, "Greg, there are things in your life that concern Me much more than cancer." The Holy Spirit began to reveal to me conditions of my heart; the pride, the stubbornness and the rebellion that existed were hindering me more than any physical infirmity.

Though I could sense nothing happening in the physical realm, I could sense that God was performing spiritual surgery, opening up areas in my life that were under a facade of denial. In the eyes of God, the condition of the heart always takes precedence over the physical condition.

The rest of the week in Tampa was a wonderful time of rest and relaxation. Rodney's ministry team treated us like royalty. The services blessed both Ronda and me, and though my physical condition was continuing to deteriorate, I sensed that God had done something marvelous in me. I had gone to the conference with the express desire of getting rid of the cancer, but instead, I left with a deep sense that God was going to do a marvelous work in my spirit. And I knew my fighting a physical infirmity was going to be the avenue He was going to use to accomplish that work.

BACK HOME AGAIN IN INDIANA

Immediately after arriving back in Indiana, I began to prepare myself mentally for surgery. The radical cystectomy and the neobladder surgery was a complicated medical procedure averaging nine to eleven hours on the operating table accompanied by a seven- to ten-day stay in the hospital. After the surgery and release from the hospital, a six-week recuperation process is required for healing and personal training for the new process of urination that the neobladder requires. It didn't seem to matter how closely I walked with God, getting prepared for all that stretched my spirituality awfully thin.

My surgery was scheduled for 6:30 A.M. Monday morning. I elected not to spend Sunday night in the hospital but to drive the one hundred thirty miles to Indianapolis the morning of the surgery. I wanted to be able to attend both services at church and give the Lord one last opportunity to spare me all the trouble and medical expense. Services were

20

wonderful that last Sunday, but there was no miracle. I was headed for surgery.

That night prior to surgery was a sleepless one. An upset stomach caused by the last round of antibiotics and an awful sense of dread and anxiety made rest impossible. By 3:30 A.M. we were on Interstate 65 headed for the IUPUI Medical Center in Indianapolis. Our conversation was limited as we both fought to maintain faith and a positive attitude that God was somehow going to work this all out for our good and His glory. (See Romans 8:28.)

Preparation for surgery was a whirlwind of activity. The last few minutes prior to my walk to the operating room were filled with consent forms being signed, IV lines being inserted, and prayer and encouragement from my family. One last time, the medical staff went over the procedure with me. I was going to have a cystectomy with continent urinary reservoir construction, a procedure where the bladder and the prostate gland are removed and a bladder is constructed from a section of the colon. I would be in surgery eight to ten hours, followed by twenty-four hours in Intensive Care, and if all went well, taken to a regular room to recuperate for ten more days.

As a precaution, they measured me for an ileal loop, a more standard urinary diversion that consists of a stoma that drains into an external bag. The ileal loop would be used only if the cancer was in areas that the CT scan had not revealed. I so distinctly remember looking at the clock in the operating room. It read 6:50 A.M., and I made a mental note that the next time I would open my eyes, it would be somewhere around 5:00 P.M. The last thing I remember prior to falling asleep was asking the presence of the Holy Spirit to surround me in the operating room.

My Definition of "Bad"
Was About to Be Revised

In what seemed like but a moment of time, I could hear my name being called. The sounds were coming from a fog that was so thick I could not see who was speaking or why they wanted me. As I struggled to respond, my eyes searched for the clock on the wall. It was 11:00 A.M. and my hand instinctively reached for my right side and felt the urostomy pouch in place. I was in a deep fog, but I had enough wits about me to realize that something had gone wrong during the surgery.

Nausea produced by the fear of the unknown swept over me like a river. I desperately needed two things: something to relieve the sickness in my stomach, and someone to tell me what had gone wrong in surgery. An anti-nausea medicine took care of the first need, and the appearance of my wife took care of the second.

Ronda has always been a fortress of strength, and rarely in our twenty-four years of marriage had I ever seen her shaken. As she held my hand and began to speak, I could feel the tremors that ran through her body. Very briefly and concisely she gave me the surgeon's report. The surgical procedure had been abandoned because of the discovery of grossly positive lymph nodes. I had been given an ileal loop, the very procedure I had gone to IUPUI to avoid. According to Dr. Rowland's vast experience, he estimated that I had six months to a year to live.

The suddenness and intensity of the news so completely stunned me that I did not know how to react. I thought that evidently God was through with me, and I would have only a limited time to close the book on my earthly existence. I was glad my life insurance policy would take care of Ronda and the kids.

All Is Well, Then Suddenly...

The rest of that Monday was a haze of voices talking around me. I vaguely remember the steady stream of family and friends, who after hearing the news, had either visited to pray for me or to comfort Ronda. I remember thinking, *This is like lying in the funeral home and seeing and hearing people talking to you and about you, but not having the ability to participate in the conversation.* I longed for a clear mind and for the effects of the powerful drugs from the surgery to subside.

What am I going to do? How am I going to handle all this? Am I really going to die?

Tuesday morning dawned, and the fog in my brain finally lifted. I could think clearly, but my reality had not changed. The cancer in my bladder had found its way into my lymphatic system, and the doctors were certain that it would only be a matter of time before it would invade my liver and lungs. I had a sixteen-inch vertical incision in my abdomen, a gastric tube down my throat, a urostomy pouch on my side, and the prognosis that my forty-fourth birthday would be my last.

The surgeon and the oncologists were scheduled to visit, and I had a list of questions to ask them. Everything I had heard had been second-hand information, and I was anxiously awaiting their visit so I could hear their prognosis first-hand. Ten minutes before their 10:00 visit, the phone rang.

STEVE MARCUM, RELUCTANT PROPHET

As I answered the call, the voice on the other end was sobbing so hard that I could not recognize the voice. The man simply kept saying, "This is Steve." I have several close friends and cousins named Steve, but finally recognized Steve as Steve Marcum, pastor of Graceland Baptist Church in New Albany, Indiana.

Steve began to shout to me, "You are not going to die! You are not going to die! It does not matter what the doctors tell you. You are not going to die!" Through his sobbing, he explained that I had not even been on his mind as he was reading his daily devotional, which happened to be 2 Kings 20 in which Hezekiah had a sickness unto death, but the Lord relented and gave Hezekiah more time.

Steve explained to me that the Holy Spirit had come upon him so strongly that he had to call and tell me that the Lord had spoken to his heart that I was going to live and not die. Our conversation was short but encouraging. Of the thousands of phone conversations I have had in my lifetime, that one call was the most unique and uplifting I have ever received.

The Holy Spirit could not have chosen an instrument that would validate His word to me more than Steve Marcum could. Steve comes from a solid and conservative Southern Baptist background and has never been given to emotional hype. If the messenger had been one of my Pentecostal buddies, I would have been concerned that they were speaking a message to me birthed more out of their desire for me to make it rather than being a spokesman for the Holy Spirit.

My conversation with Steve was the first spark of life I had felt for the past twenty-four hours. The timing of the message took on tremendous significance because, no sooner than my conversation ended with Steve, Dr. Rowland, making his morning rounds, walked into my room with a somewhat somber appearance.

WHICH REPORT TO BELIEVE?

Dr. Rowland explained to me that he had abandoned the radical cystecomy procedure because of the appearance of cancer in my lymphatic system. He had removed eighteen cancerous lymph nodes and diverted my urinary tract through an ileal loop because the tumors in my bladder were close to shutting down the normal urinary function.

Dr. Rowland is a very compassionate man, and I could tell that he preferred not to have much influence on my decision-making process. But I had to make some big decisions about future treatment, and I needed his expert medical advice. I pressed him as hard as I could to squeeze from him every detail about his view of my medical condition. From his involvement with many others who have had the degree of lymphatic involvement I had, these realities surfaced: He had never had a patient with my current medical condition live any longer than eleven months. I could have as little as two months or as much as six months to a year, according to how fast the cancer spread.

When I pressed Dr. Rowland as to what he would do if he were in my condition based on his dealings with the same scenario in others, he simply told me that he would not take the chemotherapy, "But go home, get my house in order, and enjoy what remaining time I had left." He patted my hand and left Ronda and me to mull over the devastating prognosis.

In a matter of an hour, I had received two very contrasting reports. One report was that I was going to live, and the other report was that I was going to be dead within a year. Both reports were floating around in my mind, as two oncologists from the hospital visited to give me information on what type of treatments were available. Their faces looked like talking heads as they explained to me that the standard treatment for my degree of cancer was not very promising. Only about 20 percent of patients had any response at all, and the greatest benefit from the treatment they offered was that it would simply delay the inevitable and buy me a little more time.

As they talked to me, my thoughts drifted to the images of people I had pastored who had suffered the devastating side effects of chemotherapy. The treatment had left them unable to enjoy any quality of life. I had seen enough of it that I had made up my mind a long time ago that, if faced with terminal cancer, chemotherapy would not be an option for me. I thanked the doctors for their time and told them that after I was home and able to think clearly, I would contact their office and inform them of my decision.

NO MATTER HOW DARK, LIGHT PENETRATES

Ronda and I determined that we would make the best of my ten-day hospital stay, remain as positive as possible, and not make any decisions until we got home. I needed the atmosphere of my church and friends and needed to hear clearly the voice of the Holy Spirit.

My ten-day stay at IUPUI Medical Center included my forty-fourth birthday. Although we were one hundred thirty miles from home, over fifty friends and family members visited that day loaded with gifts and cards. I was blessed with a tremendous outpouring of love that made me all the more anxious to get home and back to the church I pastored.

In spite of all the negatives going on in my life, the church I had pastored for seventeen years was having a real move of God. Since the day of my diagnosis, people had met every night at the church to pray for me and seek God's guidance for the future. As they united together to wage war for my life, the Holy Spirit fell in such a powerful way that it swept out all negativity, doubt and fear.

These precious friends of mine determined that they were going to grab hold of the altar and not let go until my recovery was certain, and in the process, spiritual renewal began to move in the body of the church, having a profound effect on everyone attending those nightly sessions. There was no doom and gloom at Grace Tabernacle, only a strong expectancy that I was going to get a miracle.

During my stay in the hospital, call after call encouraged me not to lose hope and faith but to press in to God and expect His intervention in my situation. Even with all the outward circumstances going on in my life, these calls of encouragement kept the despair from overtaking me. It seemed as if each call was perfectly timed to meet whatever mental battle I was having.

The remainder of my hospital stay was devoted to learning how to deal with a urostomy and all the care necessary to keep it functional. Wearing a bag was going to bring about some major adjustments in my lifestyle. Flanges, snap-on bags and baggy clothes would become a part of my daily existence. In the midst of these personal profound life adjustments, I was beginning to see that the Lord was taking me down a road that was going to rearrange my entire perspective on life.

The day of my release was dark, dreary and snowy, but my spirits were soaring as we drove away from the hospital. I was on my way home where I could control my environment, could seek God without interruption, and could be surrounded by family and friends. As we turned off State Highway 11 onto South Harrison Park Road toward the church, a banner caught my attention. It read, "Welcome home, Greg and Ronda."

Tears begin to fill my eyes as I looked down the entire stretch between the highway and the church, as sign after sign proclaimed not only the church's compassion for us, but also signs that proclaimed the healing power of the God we serve. I was absolutely overwhelmed with emotion.

the Lord than I had ever known.

For twelve days I had been bombarded by bad news. I had had little time to pray, read the Word, or get any kind of direction from God, yet His power and presence was like a sweet stream of refreshing. I began to pray for others, and I saw God's presence and anointing flow through me even though I had been out of spiritual commission while lying in a hospital bed. My faith began to soar and the thought that maybe God wasn't through with me began dancing around in my mind.

Hope is a precious commodity, and our faith brings us the things we hope for. Hope is future, but faith is now. Hope for my future, which had been in short supply, began to flow into the reservoir of my spirit. Suddenly, to a man who thought that he might not have a future, sprang the possibility that "with God all things are possible" (Mark 10:27, NKJV).

As I looked over those gathered in the sanctuary, I was amazed that on a snowy Tuesday evening so many had ventured out to pray for me. For all of us, life has many demands pulling at us, and most folks never lack for something to do. I kept thinking, *Why have these people given up what they wanted to do, to do something for me?*

The answer came as I looked into the eyes of several saints in a prayer circle. I realized that during that season in their lives, they loved me more than they loved themselves. What a powerful revelation, that just as Jesus loved us more than He loved himself, so the Church was loving me and putting me ahead of their own needs.

There is power in our lives only to the degree that we are willing to give it up. If we want to find our life, we must lose it. (See Matthew 16:25.) God's power and presence is manifested when people put others' needs ahead of their own. If we love others more than ourselves, we are displaying the form of love that motivated Jesus to be nailed to a cross.

God moved mightily through the obedience of Jesus Christ. Jesus could have come down from the cross any time He wanted, but His loving others more than Himself produced a moving of the hand of God that resulted in the salvation of anyone who would believe. I am firmly convinced that when we love others more than ourselves, we will see God move in our churches as never before.

NEVER UNDERESTIMATE THE POWER OF EXHORTATION

A barrage of cards of encouragement arrived daily in the mailbox, and mail time became the highlight of my day. It seemed that every time I would begin to get discouraged, just the right card from the right person would brighten my world. The Bible tells us to encourage one another (see Hebrews 10:25), and I was so glad that people from all walks of life and from varying church backgrounds took time to think of me and send an expression of their care and concern for my situation. Many days those cards helped me through a difficult day.

Finances poured in from everywhere, meeting all our medical obligations. Family, friends and churches were determined that my medical expenses would not put us in a financial bind. We received several gifts from people we had never met, but who had heard about what we were going through. Our church, Grace Tabernacle, gave us an offering totaling several thousand dollars to pay for things our insurance would not cover.

Other churches in the area sent us checks to be used for whatever was needed. Graceland Baptist Church, where my friend Steve Marcum pastored, called and offered whatever financial assistance I might need to pay any balance during my hospitalization. The local church community immersed

CHAPTER 2

Difficult Decisions

O VERWHELMED IS AN inadequate adjective to describe the rush of emotions that engulfed me as we drove to the church. The ill effects of a twelve-day stay in the hospital seemed to vanish as I read banner after banner proclaiming God's love and concern for my situation.

It was after 9:00 P.M. on a Tuesday, yet the parking lot at the church was full of cars. I convinced Ronda to stop, but only after promising we would just sneak in the back door, go upstairs, and look into the sanctuary from the sound room.

As we walked in the back door, I could hear the cries of intercession and shouts of praise flowing from the sanctuary. The intensity of their prayers completely overruled any thoughts of negativity and defeat. Those dear saints prayed fervently for my complete victory. From no closer than the hallway, I felt a charge of spiritual renewal that energized my faith.

Nothing could have kept me from joining in with what was happening in the sanctuary that night. Tears blinded me as I joined my spirit with those who interceded for me. In my entire Christian experience, that memory is forever etched as the time I felt more love from family, friends and us with a practical outpouring of compassion. Ronda and I were absolutely overwhelmed and relieved, knowing we had one less thing on our overloaded minds.

THE TIDE BEGINS TO TURN

We were given a six-week window until a return trip to the hospital was needed for another CT scan. I was assured by the doctors that by that visit the tests would show that the disease had spread to my liver and lungs, and if I chose to look into the chemotherapy options again, a proposed regimen of drugs would be discussed.

Every day had become precious, and I wanted to enjoy it to the fullest. I love to preach and was determined to do so. I arrived home on Tuesday and immediately began to prepare to preach Wednesday night. I had a large incision in my abdomen and was adjusting to the urostomy bag on my right side, so I decided to modify my normal preaching attire. I purchased a couple of jogging suits, put on a T-shirt and tennis shoes, tucked my Bible under my arm and headed for church, determined to preach as long as I had breath and could still sit up and take nourishment. The church purchased a large blue recliner and put it on the platform for me to sit in until it was time to deliver the evening message. This arrangement might not have been very traditional, but it sure worked for me.

During the six-week window, the congregation at Grace Tabernacle met every night to pray for my healing. No matter what kind of day I had experienced, those nightly meetings became a life-sustaining experience for me. Nightly, my spirit was inundated with God's concern for me through the people as they prayed for me. Romans 10:17 says, "Faith comes by hearing, and hearing by the word of God" (NKJV). Faith for my healing would rise in me as friends read aloud the promises of God concerning my situation.

As Dickens once wrote, "It was the best of times and the worst of times." Daily I went from the battlefield to the spiritual hospital, from times of struggle to times of refreshing. I discovered, as did the apostle Paul, that power is perfected in weakness and that when we are weak is when we are strong. (See 2 Corinthians 12:9–10.) Invitations to speak began to pour in from Baptist, Christian, Independent and Assemblies of God churches in the area. To my utmost amazement, I witnessed God's power displayed everywhere I went, and I operated under the greatest anointing I had ever experienced. I would have a tough day, feeling so bad that it was hard to pray and prepare to minister. Then when I would go to church and open my mouth to speak, a rush of the presence of God flowed that I knew was completely His doing and not my own.

It was such a paradox to me that during the toughest time of my life, God would use me the most. I discovered that the anointing of God is all about Him and His desire to help people and very little about the vessel He is using. We are like a hose from which the Spirit flows. We just need to keep our hose free from any spiritual debris that would hinder the flow of the Holy Spirit.

THE DOOR YOU CLOSE MAY BE THE DOOR GOD WANTS YOU TO WALK THROUGH

The six-week window closed faster than I anticipated. I was not looking forward to the CT scan and its revelations, but somehow I found the courage to make the trip to Indianapolis and hand my body over to the doctors to be poked and prodded again. I determined not to let anything get to me. I guarded my emotions to fortify myself against negative doctors' reports because I found that if my emotions got involved, I would be ineffective in making a spiritual decision. I wanted to make all decisions based on what I felt the Holy Spirit was saying to me, not on the dictates of my emotions.

Though I was braced for the worst, the CT scan revealed the cancer had *not* spread to the liver and lungs, and the doctors were encouraged that the disease had not spread as rapidly as they had anticipated. I was nonetheless assured that it was only a matter of time before the natural progression of the disease would reach those vital organs. The inevitable would not be avoided, only delayed.

While the doctors were discussing what my medical options were, I could not help but think about the six-week season of prayer that my congregation had engaged in on my behalf. *Was it possible that those nights of intercession had stopped the progression of the disease? Was it within the realm of hope that God was intervening on my behalf and touching me with His life-altering power?*

I felt a great sense of relief that things were, at least, not getting worse. A stalemate is better than an advance of the enemy anytime. Dr. Rowland, my urologist, wanted me to meet with Dr. Bruce Roth, an oncologist who specialized in cancer of the urinary tract to consider chemotherapy options. The FDA had approved some drugs to be tested on bladder cancer, and the hospital was going to be part of a nationwide program to study the effects of these drugs on terminally ill patients or on patients with a prognosis of having less than a year to live.

Chemotherapy, for a multitude of reasons, had very little appeal to me. I had conducted too many funerals of cancer victims who had received little help from the oncologists' valiant efforts to stop the spread of this deadly disease through a regimen of chemotherapy. Most of us have made predetermined decisions about what we would or would not do in the event of contracting a serious illness. Too often those decisions are based on a view from the outside looking in instead of from the inside looking out. Though I had said, "Never" to ever consider taking chemotherapy, my circumstances caused my never attitude to change.

My biggest concern was what effects the drugs would have on my ability to preach. In viewing my options, I determined that I would rather have six months of quality time, able to perform my duties as a pastor, than have one year of existence lying around in bed overwhelmed by the effects of the chemotherapy. I did not want to do anything that would steal any quality time from me.

Anyone combating cancer will tell you that making decisions about what kind and how much of any treatment offered is a gut-wrenching battle. Your decisions not only affect you, but everyone around you. So many lives—your spouse's, children's and friends'—are drastically altered by whatever decision you make. Until a decision is made, sifting through all the options consumes every waking moment.

After being worn down by the constant encourage-ment of family and friends for me to meet with Dr. Bruce Roth, I reluctantly agreed to at least hear what he had to offer. By that time in my fight with cancer, I had developed a rather dim view of hospitals and doctors. The prospect of a three-hour drive combined with a lengthy wait in a doctor's office to meet with someone I really did not want to see produced a preacher with a nasty attitude. The thing I dreaded the most was hearing, once again, how bad my condition was.

My expectations of hearing a negative report were ful-filled as I listened to one of Dr. Roth's interns go over my medical chart. She explained that the possible chemo reg-imen would not cure me, but only give me an uncertain possibility of retarding the growth of the tumors. Case studies had shown that 40 percent of cancer patients taking the regimen of drugs they wanted to give me had some positive response. I was assured that, within the realm of the medical field, the chemotherapy was my first and last option for treatment. If I decided not to take the drugs, or if I took them and had no response, my life span would be measured in months, not years.

My foul disposition heightened. The visit was every bit as bad and worse than I had imagined it would be, and I was on the verge of leaving when Dr. Roth entered the examination room. With no fanfare, and after a simple introduction, Dr. Roth asked me two questions. One, "Would you like to be able to preach another year?" And two, "Would you like to see your son play another year of baseball?" Both, he explained, could be possible if I would give chemo a chance.

The regimen Dr. Roth prescribed would have some very serious side effects, but in his medical opinion, the drugs would not interfere with my pastoral duties. Dr. Bruce Roth could sell an ice cube to an Eskimo, and his endearing personality and positive attitude caused me to totally change my perspective. There would be no guarantees, but a 40 percent chance was better than no chance at all.

The drugs that Dr. Roth wanted to give me had been proven effective in treatment of some types of cancer but had never been used in the treatment of bladder cancer. He wanted me to be a part of a study group of twenty-four patients who would be given a combination of three drugs that would be compared to other patients receiving differing combinations of other recently approved FDA drugs. Resulting responses would be compared, and hopefully, something that would help enhance the length and quality of the lives of cancer patients would emerge from the studies. I could not help but feel we were being asked to become guinea pigs in the medical field's quest for new knowledge.

The regimen required each patient to receive chemo intravenously in six different five-day hospital stays. I would arrive at the cancer ward on Monday morning, get hooked up, and receive the cancer fighting drugs and other medicines to combat the side effects of the chemo. On Friday evenings after each five-day stay, I would return home to rest and prepare for the next round of chemo sixteen days later.

April through July, my life would revolve around a twenty-one-day cycle: five days in the hospital and sixteen days at home. The only positive element was that after two sessions, the doctors would be able to determine if the drugs were having any success; if they were not, the treatment would be stopped.

I left Dr. Roth's office with a myriad of things floating through my mind. Family and friends encouraged me to take the chemo. I despised the thought of giving my body over to the doctors again and putting my hope in their abilities, but the impassioned pleas from those who loved me started to wear on my resistance. Night after night, prayer session after prayer session, I agonized over what decision to make. I wanted the peace of God to be my umpire on this matter (see Colossians 3:15), but finding that peace became a lengthy ordeal.

One factor that heavily influenced my decision was a Trinity Broadcasting Network telecast interviewing several pastors and spiritual leaders who had overcome cancer. As each one shared their ordeals of surgery, chemotherapy and radiation, as well as the emotional and spiritual battles they had survived, I began to weep as I listened to others who could relate to the feelings of my infirmities.

As those pastors and spiritual leaders shared their

experiences with chemo, each proclaimed that they had continued to minister during treatment. Hope began to well up within me as I saw survivors of the very disease I was battling proclaim victory on the other side of treatment.

After several times of intense prayer, and weighing every factor over and over, I decided to take the chemotherapy. The best-case scenario would give me some more quality time, and the worst-case scenario would be that I had at least exhausted all my options for a possible medical cure.

Before chemo could begin, the tumors in my bladder would have to be measured so that a standard of the effectiveness of the drugs could be determined. If the tumors diminished in size, the doctors would know the drugs were working. If the tumors did not respond or continued to enlarge, the treatments would be determined to be ineffective and then stopped. A cystoscope performed three days before my first scheduled chemo session revealed three golf ball-sized tumors in my bladder. The tumors were measured and photographed, and those pictures became the *markers* that would determine the effectiveness of the chemotherapy. My journey into the unknown of chemotherapy was just beginning.

CHAPTER 3

Confronting My Situation

E VEN THOUGH IT is inevitable that we all are one day going to die, having a time frame placed on that inevitable event brings a stark realism that instantly sobers you. The realism I faced that cold February afternoon sitting alone in my office was that unless something supernatural happened to me, I was going to die. As is the case with so many decisions in life when the going gets tough and it looks like all is over, we must decide what course of action we are going to take. Will we give in to the voices of despondency that scream in our head and the video effects that our eyes see, or will we rise to "fight the good fight of faith" (1 Timothy 6:12, NKJV)?

With simple determination and no emotions, I decided that I was going to fight the good fight of faith to my final breath. Either God was going to help me, or I was going to die, but either way, whatever time I had left was not going to be lived feeling sorry for myself and under the control of discouragement and fear. I needed a battle plan to refer to on a daily basis to keep focused on the truth and the reality of the God I serve.

Almost daily, either by personal visit, mail or telephone, I received videotapes and articles about alternative cancer treatment or pamphlets about diets that fight cancer cells. As this stuff piled up on my desk in front of me, the thought occurred, *It would take me a year to go through all this stuff, and I only have six months to live. I am not going to spend the bulk of my remaining time wading through this pile, hoping to find a cure hidden somewhere in all of this.*

The Bible presents Jesus in many different reflections of the Godhead. He is the exact representation of God according to Hebrews 1:3. If you want to know what God is like, simply look to the Jesus in the Gospels. Jesus is the exact representation of the Father. As I looked at all the envelopes, brochures, books and tapes laying on my desk, I wondered if there was anyone who could really relate to what I was going through. I did not need theory or experimentation. I needed reality—someone who had gone through what I was currently battling and had survived. Jesus is touched with the feeling of our infirmities (see Hebrews 4:15), and on that day, not only did I need a Savior who was touched with the feelings of my infirmities, but I also needed encouragement from someone who had fought cancer and won.

As I began to sort through the pile of information on my desk, I came across *Healed of Cancer*, a little book by Dodie Osteen. As I picked up the book from the pile on my desk, a flicker of hope, something I desperately needed, ignited in my spirit. I sat down on my couch and began to read the fascinating story of her initial diagnosis, ensuing battle, and ultimate victory over liver cancer. The thing that most impressed me was the battle plan she devised containing scriptures and attitudes of the heart that she reviewed daily to keep her faith strong in God's ultimate victory.

Please understand what I am about to say, because I believe it is true. Unless you have gone through something, though you may have knowledge concerning it, you have little to say to someone who is going through something you have never experienced. I was constantly bombarded by well-meaning people who told me what they thought I should do. Reality for all of us is that we really do not know what we will do in any given situation until we are there. I found myself, during my battle with cancer, doing things that I had once proclaimed I would never do.

This is one reason that Jesus had to come to earth as a human being. (See John 1:14.) He had to be touched with the feelings of our infirmities if He was to be able to fulfill His present-day office as intercessor. (See Hebrews 7:25.) Because He has gone before us in all the realities of life's experiences, He can come to the aid of those who are struggling. I found myself gravitating to people who had already battled cancer and alienated myself from all the theories of those who did not have first-hand experience with what I was going through.

I placed my trash can beside my desk and, with one swoop, eliminated the pile of material on my desk. I retrieved those materials born from real experiences and placed them next to my Bible. I needed a battle plan, and it was going to have to come from the Word of God interspersed with the real experiences of those who had faced cancer and survived.

I sat down at my word processor that February afternoon, and the following thoughts, attitudes and scriptures became my daily battle plan that sustained me. The battle plan was birthed from the Word of God, my own failures up to that point in battling cancer, and the testimonies and successes of others who had overcome cancer. The plan included the following:

Remain positive. Negativity will destroy you.

During my nine-day stay in the hospital, the only news we heard was bad news. I had gone into surgery to have my cancerous bladder replaced with a neobladder, but came out of surgery with a urostomy pouch. Because of grossly positive lymph node involvement surrounding my bladder, a prognosis that the disease had most likely invaded my liver and lungs gave a life expectancy of two months to a year. Believe me, it takes creative thinking to find anything positive in that prognosis.

When we arrived home, we began to receive phone calls and visits from family and friends who wanted to know the seriousness of my condition. Day after day, our conversations were consumed with relating the negative prognosis we were given.

Phone call after phone call, visit after visit focused on the negative. A depression set in like I had never experienced.

Every night, I would wake up around 3 A.M. with the same dream. Pallbearers, representing both sides of my family and close friends, carried me down the aisle of the church. I was overwhelmed by the idea that I was going to die. One evening during that time, Ronda came running down the stairs to the couch where I was sleeping and threw herself on me and began to weep uncontrollably with the thought of my impending death.

I made a determination that night that Ronda and I were going to get out of the realm of the negative and get into the realm of the positive. We both determined that we were not going to give any expression to negativism. We realized that positive confession was not going to make the cancer go away, but positive confession was going to help our attitudes tremendously.

The Bible tells us we are not to be conformed to this world, shaped by outward circumstances and influences, but to be transformed by the renewing of our minds. (See Romans 12:2.) I understood the principle that the Holy Spirit speaks to our renewed born-again spirit, not our unregenerate mind. I desperately needed to quit listening to my thoughts and start listening to what the Spirit of

God was telling me.

Ronda and I determined from that day forth that we were going to respond positively to everyone who asked about my condition. We were not going to lie but respond in such a manner that would keep us focused on what we believed God was going to do, not what the doctors said was inevitable.

We could not believe what a change speaking positively made. I found that speaking to myself more and listening to my head less brought hope and life. I could not sit around all day and dwell on negative things and not expect it to drain all the life out of me. To stay positive, you must devise a plan and determine to carry it out.

Let the peace of God be your greatest source of guidance.

In a struggle with cancer, there will be many important decisions to be made. Advice to battle cancer came from every conceivable avenue. Some close friends told me that seeking any more medical treatment would show a lack of faith and would cause me to lose my connection to God's healing power. Others told me to seek every available medical treatment whether FDA approved or not. Friends who had read articles on diets encouraged me to change my eating habits. Relatives who cared deeply for me told me of experimental treatments available in Mexico and Europe. I was flooded with information and at a total loss as to what to do.

Many times in life we cannot see the forest for the trees, especially when our vision is completely blocked by a large oak that is so large it encompasses all we can see. We do not know what to do, but God does. The Scripture proclaims, "if any of you lacks wisdom, let him ask of God, who gives to all liberally" (James 1:5, NKJV). It was my experience that

I did not know what to do or what avenue to take until the exact moment the decision had to be made. I learned to live on a daily basis, asking God's guidance for that day's decision, and not to concern myself about future events. I took to heart the admonition of the scripture that tells me to take no thought about tomorrow because "each day has enough trouble of its own" (Matthew 6:34, NCV).

In my struggle with cancer, I discovered that I must do whatever I felt peace in my heart to do. There will be voices screaming everywhere, and the one that screams the loudest might not be the right one. I found that following only those things that were birthed of peace produced life.

Never sit around and feel sorry for yourself.

Pity never wins. As I have pastored people over the years, I have counseled many who have struggled with depression and discouragement. I have been able to help some of them, but I could not reach others. I knew that one of the major battles I was going to face was the strong desire to give in to depression and discouragement: *Why do I have to go through this? I have faithfully served God in ministry for nearly twenty years and this is my reward?* These questions dogged me constantly.

Over the years I have observed that those who give in to depression usually begin by regressing or pulling away from others. They like to stay home, pull the blinds and invite into their living room all the little devils that have been harassing them. If you invite the enemy in for a pity party, he will bring all his bells and whistles. The enemy will always bring old home movies that highlight the times you have felt rejected and unloved by people and God.

The commercials in the home movies stress how dire your situation is, and how there is no hope, and that you might as well give up. An afternoon pity party in the

43

company of devils usually entails a double or triple feature. Every negative thought is played over and over, each time allowing the scenario to get worse and worse. The end result is that pity and sorrow become your constant companions. You lose all your strength and energy as the weight of your circumstances, defined by demonic forces, crushes you with waves of despair and despondency. Your isolation separates you from anything encouraging or godly. Pity has become your master.

I came to the conclusion that the answer was not in my head. There is nothing rational about cancer. I began to force myself out of the house and among people. I knew I could either feel bad lying around the house, or I could feel bad mingling with church friends and family. My countenance began to change by my being around people and hearing positive comments. I understood the seriousness of time alone for prayer and meditation, but I stopped sitting around the house thinking about my condition. I jumped into the flow of life and found the battle with self-pity one that I could overcome.

Don't allow your imagination to run wild.

The Bible tells us that "though we walk in the flesh, we do not war according to the flesh" (2 Corinthians 10:3–5, NKJV). The weapons of our warfare are divinely powerful for the destruction of fortresses. These strongholds are vain imaginations, foolish speculations and every lofty thing that exalts itself against the true knowledge of God. We must remember that all communication with the Lord comes from the Spirit of God who reveals things to our spirits.

The Holy Spirit will illuminate to us what the Spirit of God is saying. Our head plays no role in this communication. Our spirits will feed our head one dose of reality at a time. But transformation comes to any person as his mind is renewed as the Spirit feeds it the truth of God. I had to learn to take negative thoughts captive and cast them down.

After casting down the negative thoughts, I had to speak to my mind the truth about my condition, speaking to myself more and listening to myself less. One thing I found that helped greatly was finding a quiet place to talk aloud to myself. I had to speak to myself louder than my mind was talking to me. Some of the best sermons I have ever preached were to myself as I cast down vain imaginations and foolish speculations and replaced them with the all-powerful Word of God.

Do not focus all your attention and energies on yourself.

It is our natural tendency when fighting a giant like cancer to focus all our attention and energies on ourselves. However, when we get our minds exclusively on ourselves and our needs, we begin to weaken. There are all kinds of natural laws that govern the universe. The law of gravity tells us that what goes up must come down. All of us have discovered that no two pieces of matter can occupy the same place at the same time. We all have experienced a knock or two on the head that has made that law a painful reality.

Spiritual laws are no different than natural laws. There are God-given principles that govern life in the spirit realm. One of those laws is the law of sowing and reaping. Luke, the apostle tells us that if we give, it will be given back to us in such a good measure that we will not be able to contain it. (See Luke 6:38.)

One of the biggest mistakes I made in the early stages of my illness was that I focused too much attention on my own need and too little on the needs of those around me. Desperately desiring for the stranglehold of depression to be broken, I asked the Lord why I could not shake its powerful grip. Like so many times during my ordeal, the Holy Spirit illuminated my mind to see that I was not giving anything out. If nothing is being planted, there can never be any harvest.

With this revelation, I decided to throw myself into ministry with both barrels blazing. Our church services were not going to revolve around my sickness, but the needs of the congregation were going to take precedence over mine. I determined to focus my attention on others who were hurting and give what I could to them. I found that as I prayed and ministered to others, I felt dramatically different about my own circumstances. As I gave ministry to others, the Holy Spirit ministered peace and encouragement to me in a far greater fashion than I had experienced by focusing my attention upon myself. I found that if you give out of your need, God causes good things to come your way.

You cannot lie around sick.

You must do everything possible to stay active and productive. You must not give in to the sickness. Believe me, I know this sounds harsh, but this truth is forged in the fires of adversity. In 1996, I had two major surgeries, six separate five-day chemotherapy treatments, and spent fifty days in the hospital. Much of what I faced was dealing with thoughts telling me to just give in, lie down and take it easy.

I made a mental commitment to be up and around as much as possible. I learned how to pace myself because the chemo took a terrible toll on my physical strength. I would work at the office until my strength was gone. Afternoon naps became a necessity.

My chemotherapy was on a twenty-one-day cycle, arriving at the hospital early Monday morning, getting hooked up to an IV and taking the drugs until Friday afternoon. I was allowed to go home for sixteen days while my body recovered, then start the cycle all over again.

It always amazed me that the day I felt the worst was also the day I had the most to do. Sunday was a tough day. Most Sundays during the chemo treatments, I found myself nauseous and physically weak. Every round of chemo left me a little weaker and with less resilience to bounce back. During the first four rounds of treatment, I never missed a service. I would sit in the blue recliner near the platform to conserve my strength for preaching and ministry to the church.

It was the Sunday morning after my fifth round of chemo that I hit a wall. When Ronda called for me to get up, I told her that I just could not make it. I was too sick. I felt that surely everyone would understand that I, of all people, deserved to lie around and take it easy. As I snuggled under the covers, the Holy Spirit quietly spoke these words to my heart, "So this is where you draw the line. This is how sick you have to be to lie down and quit? If this is where you draw the line, the devil will keep you at this place and render you ineffective." As this sobering piece of revelation hit me, I jumped out of bed and headed for the shower. I had come too far to lie down and quit.

Too many people facing adversity lie down and quit way too early in the fracas. If you tell the enemy where the line is, he will manipulate circumstances to keep you there at that point of pain or discomfort or mental anguish. You must determine that as long as you have physical strength, you must stay productive. This attitude of the heart is more for your benefit than for the benefit for others.

Stay mentally strong by renewing your mind on a daily basis.

Allow your spirit to renew your mind on a daily basis. There is something about the twenty-four-hour cycle of life that many of us have never fully comprehended. If we understand that we cannot live on yesterday's food or water, why do we think we can live on yesterday's spiritual revelations?

If I did not renew my mind daily by feeding on the Word of God and His promises, discouragement and depression would begin to creep out of the shadows to engulf me in darkness. Your mind will begin to waver and you will be prone to believe the negative. But if you keep your spirit strong, it will speak spiritual realities to your head and bring it back to the realm of faith. You must keep your spirit strong, or your head will waver. James 1:8 warns us about the danger of being double-minded. The Word of God must become the source of your strength. You must read, meditate and confess the realities of God's Word on a daily basis.

In spite of what your eyes see, your ears hear and your thoughts proclaim, you must have absolute faith that the Word of God cannot lie. The writer of Hebrews cautions us to "hold fast the confession of our hope without wavering, for He who promised is faithful" (Hebrews 10:23, NKJV). Your grip on God is your faith. His grip on you is His grace. As you meditate on His Word, your grip on God will increase. You must hear the right things even if you have to read the Word aloud so you can hear yourself proclaim words of faith inspired by the Holy Spirit.

State your case before God.

One thing every born-again believer must fully realize is that he has access to the throne room of God. (See Hebrews 10:19–20.) We have access because God personally made Himself responsible for our sinful condition in Adam. He made Jesus, who knew no sin, become sin on our behalf so that we might be able to attain right standing with God. We serve a Savior who is touched with the feelings of our infirmities and invites us to the throne room to find mercy in our time of need. Through the death, burial, and resurrection of Jesus, all the barriers to God have been removed. We have been granted entrance to present ourselves to God holy, blameless and beyond reproach, wondrously transformed by our faith in His promise.

Isaiah 43:25–26 encourages us to state our case before God. I must admit that when I came across this powerful concept, I found it hard to grasp how a human being could actually relate to God in such a powerful way. As I prayed one afternoon, the stories of Moses contending with God concerning the Hebrews and Abraham contending with God over the cities of Sodom and Gomorrah flashed through my mind. I did not need to guide Israel or intercede over the fate of thousands in those cities, but I reasoned, if these men contended with God, so could I.

During my daily prayer times, I began to state my case before God. I would cry out to the Lord that seventeen years earlier He had led me to pioneer an Assembly of God church in an area that had been devoid of anything that hinted of Pentecostalism. For seventeen years I had proclaimed Him as a healer of sick bodies. I had conducted healing crusades in the church and had seen many miracles. I would contend with the Lord and ask Him how my death would glorify His name, especially in the area where I pastored. I asked Him what it would look like if I, the pastor of the local Pentecostal church who proclaimed God as healer, died little by little in front of the entire community.

The prospect of physically deteriorating in full view of our small closed community was a scenario that I told God I did not want to happen. As I would pray, I would ask God to allow me to live and not die. I asked that He would reveal to all who observed my condition that God was indeed a healer.

I would tell the Lord that my son, sixteen at the time,

needed me. My wife and daughter needed me. I was too young to die. There was too much stuff for me to do here. I told the Lord that I completely understood that Heaven was a wonderful place, but it was my desire to further His kingdom here on earth. I would promise the Lord that if He would heal me, I would continue to preach the gospel and minister to broken people through the power of His name.

I truly established in my heart the scriptural admonition that whatever things you desire, believe you shall receive them and they shall be yours. (See Mark 11:24.) I wanted to live for the glory of God, to remain with my family, and to continue to preach the gospel. I wanted to choose life and not death and reveal to all who were watching my condition that the God I served was indeed a mighty God. I cannot describe to any person the closeness I developed with the Lord as I prayed. It was as if I finally became aware of the close-knit relationship a man could have with God. I felt that, for the first time in my life, my will became intertwined with His.

Examine your heart regularly and keep it pure with God and others.

You cannot deal with the *Why me?* question twenty-four hours a day. The *Why me?* question is simply answered by understanding man's condition in Adam after the fall, or the introduction of sin. Adam's sin affected every realm of nature and humanity. Sickness is part of the package we all inherited through our ancestor Adam.

Jesus, addressing man's condition in Adam, came to earth and exhibited total dominion over sickness and disease. Sickness is a result of the fall of man, and Jesus is God's response to man's fall. He came as a Savior to save us from the consequences of sin. (See 1 John 3:8.) There is healing in Jesus' name.

I found it very easy to fall into guilt and condemnation over my condition. I constantly asked the questions, "Am I in some kind of sin that brought sickness to me?" "Have I failed God in some areas of my life and this is the punishment for it?" "Is God trying to get my attention about something?" I felt that if I could answer the *Why me?* question, everything else would fall into place.

The enemy's main weapon against us is accusation. He is described as the accuser of the brethren before God day and night. (See Revelation 12:10.) Our access to God comes through the avenue of the righteousness Jesus purchased for us. It does not come through obedience to the law.

If you are born-again, you are as righteous as you will ever get. You have right standing with God through your faith that Jesus' death, burial and resurrection satisfied all the legal demands of a holy God. You have a legal right to stand before God, not through the means of your own goodness, but fully confident that Jesus reconciled you back to the Father through His fleshly body to present you holy and blameless and beyond reproach.

I came to the spiritual reality that the enemy wanted to separate me from the Father through accusation. The enemy wanted me to be offended with God because I was sick and it was taking so long to get well. I had thought, *What kind of God would allow this to happen? I didn't deserve this.* Without my being fully aware of it, my relationship with God was slowly being poisoned and tainted because of listening to the accusations of the devil.

If there is one person in your life with whom you need a good relationship, it is God. You cannot get offended with the source of your help. Subtly, the enemy was trying to separate me from the One who holds the power of life and death.

Physical problems affect every area of our lives. No

matter how close you try to walk with God, sickness makes it difficult to focus on spiritual realities. We soon become moved only by how we feel. It is easy for attitudes to go south, and for faith and hope to dissipate. My going before the Father and allowing the Holy Spirit to examine my heart to see if there was any wicked way in me allowed His blood to cleanse me from all defilement.

Your hope is in God and those you love. You must keep those relationships open, clean and pure because everything you need for life is found there. You cannot allow how you feel physically to contaminate the pipeline from which life-sustaining sustenance flows.

Even when the physical illness begins to wear on you with the overwhelming temptation to give in to it, you will find that God is always faithful. I wavered at times almost to the point of giving up, but God would arrange someone or some thought to bring me back to the place of faith. There will be times when we waver in our minds, but our spirits must stay full of faith for our healing.

CHAPTER 4

Daily Living According to Scripture

T HE WORD OF God must become your life as you battle cancer. The answers you so desperately need, the encouragement to cope and the strength to overcome are found in God's Word. First Corinthians 2:10–16 tells us "we have the mind of Christ" (NKJV).

Too often, many among us believe that the answer for everything is found within the realm of rationality. Nothing about disease can be figured out in the mind. You can fix a flat tire or bake a cake using the carnal mind, but if you need something miraculous, such as healing, the answers are spiritual ones. These answers can only come to your spirit when you are in communion with the Spirit of God.

We must allow Scripture to determine who we are. All "faith comes by hearing, and hearing by the word of God" (Romans 10:17, NKJV). Faith is your connection to God, and the more the Word of God becomes alive in you, the more your faith will grow. The Word became my life.

Jesus had been wounded for my transgressions, bruised for my iniquities, and the chastening for my well-being had fallen on Him. By His stripes I am healed. (See Isaiah 53:5.) God is no respecter of persons. If "Jesus...is the same yesterday, today, and forever," then that same Jesus who healed disease on the shores of Galilee can heal me today. (See Hebrews 13:8, NKJV.)

The Word of God has to dwell in you, and you must speak to yourself constantly concerning the truth as recorded in the Scriptures. You must stand on the truth that you have bold access to God through the blood of Jesus; you must go to the throne room of God and confidently state your case before the Father.

Many evenings in the sanctuary of the church, I would enter into God's presence and state my case and contend with Him about my condition. "I do not want to die, but live and proclaim the glory of the Lord!" I would cry. "My wife, family and church need me."

The Lord is good and a very present help in times of trouble. As I meditated on the Word, I became aware that the same Spirit that raised Jesus from the dead was working in me and giving life to my mortal body. (See Romans 8:11.) It began to burn in my spirit that when I prayed whatever things I asked for I would receive if I prayed in faith. I developed a rock solid confidence in the integrity of the Word of God. I had to learn to not throw away my confidence, but to continue to believe, so my faith would open to me all the things God had purchased for me in Christ.

It is imperative that you get control of your thinking. You must take every thought captive to the obedience of Christ. Negative thinking is detrimental to developing faith. You must force yourself to think on the truth of God, not in doctor's reports. As the Israelites were positioned to enter their Promised Land, they had to choose between two reports—a faith-filled report from Caleb and Joshua, or a fear-filled report from ten others. (See Numbers 13 and 14.) I, too, had to choose to believe the report of the Word of God and not doctors.

Pride has no place in a battle with cancer. I knew that

there would be times when others would have to carry me. On a regular basis, the leadership of the church prayed for me. I stood on the promise of the Word of God that the effectual, fervent prayers of righteous men would play a part in the healing process. (See James 5:16.) Everywhere I went I opened myself to righteous people of God who wanted to lay hands on me and pray for my recovery.

Daily I had to check the condition of my heart. It is so easy to allow discouragement and wrong attitudes to creep in. I asked the Lord to examine the condition of my heart and deal with anything that would defile and keep His life-giving Spirit from flowing through me. I found that the negativity that was always lurking in the background was forced to stay there as I asked the Lord to allow the words of my mouth and the meditations of my heart to be acceptable in His sight.

Our lives are truly hidden with God in Christ. Nothing would calm the raging storm within like the nightly sessions I had with the Lord in the sanctuary of the church. It was there that I presented myself to God and asked for His Spirit to cleanse my entire body, soul and spirit.

During every preceding twenty-four hours, anxiety, doubt, fear and worry began to try to assert dominance over me. Nightly these attitudes had to be confronted and taken care of according to the Word of God. Demonic spirits that had been competing for my attention all day had to be driven away as I proclaimed my intentions and stated my case before God. As I would leave the church each evening, I would feel cleansed, much like a physical shower refreshes the body, but fully aware that I would have to repeat this process again the following evening.

The following scriptures I reviewed on a daily basis:

> Bless (affectionately, gratefully praise) the Lord, O my soul; and all that is [deepest] within me, bless His holy

name! Bless (affectionately, gratefully praise) the Lord,
O my soul; and forget not [one of] all his benefits—
Who forgives [every one of] all your iniquities, Who
heals [each one of] all your diseases.

—PSALM 103:1–3, AMP

But He was wounded for our transgressions, He was
bruised for our guilt and iniquities; the chastisement
[needful to obtain] peace and well-being for us was
upon Him, and with the stripes [that wounded] Him
we are healed and made whole.

—ISAIAH 53:5, AMP

I, even I, am He Who blots out and cancels your transgressions, for My own sake, and I will not remember
your sins. Put Me in remembrance [remind Me of your
merits]; let us plead and argue together. Set forth your
case, that you may be justified (proved right).

—ISAIAH 43:25–26, AMP

And He went about all Galilee, teaching in their syna-
gogues and preaching the good news (Gospel) of the
kingdom, and healing every disease and every weakness and infirmity among the people.

—MATTHEW 4:23, AMP

And Jesus said to him, What do you want Me to do for
you? And the blind man said to Him, Master, let me
receive my sight. And Jesus said to him, Go your way;
your faith has healed you. And at once he received his
sight and accompanied Jesus on the road.

—MARK 10:51–52, AMP

Is anyone among you sick? He should call in the church
elders (the spiritual guides). And they should pray over
him, anointing him with oil in the Lord's name. And
the prayer [that is] of faith will save him who is sick, and
the Lord will restore him; and if he has committed sins,
he will be forgiven.

—JAMES 5:14–15, AMP

I shall not die but live, and shall declare the works and recount the illustrious acts of the Lord.
—PSALM 118:17, AMP

Give, and [gifts] will be given to you; good measure, pressed down, shaken together, and running over, will they pour into [the pouch formed by] the bosom [of your robe and used as a bag]. For with the measure you deal out [with the measure you use when you confer benefits on others], it will be measured back to you.
—LUKE 6:38, AMP

Let the word [spoken by] Christ (the Messiah) have its home [in your hearts and minds] and dwell in you in [all its] richness; as you teach and admonish and train one another in all insight and intelligence and wisdom [in spiritual things, and as you sing] psalms and hymns and spiritual songs, making melody to God with [His] grace in your hearts.
—COLOSSIANS 3:16, AMP

The Lord is good, a Strength and Stronghold in the day of trouble; He knows (recognizes, has knowledge of, and understands) those who take refuge and trust in Him.
—NAHUM 1:7, AMP

There failed no part of any good thing which the Lord had promised to the house of Israel; all came to pass.
—JOSHUA 21:45, AMP

And if the Spirit of Him Who raised up Jesus from the dead dwells in you, [then] He Who raised up Christ Jesus from the dead will also restore to life your mortal (short-lived, perishable) bodies through His Spirit Who dwells in you.
—ROMANS 8:11, AMP

For as many as are the promises of God; they all find their Yes [answer] in Him [Christ]. For this reason we also utter the Amen (so be it) to God through Him [in

His person and by His agency] to the glory of God.
—2 CORINTHIANS 1:20, AMP

And behold, a leper came up to Him and, prostrating himself, worshiped Him, saying, Lord, if you are willing, You are able to cleanse me by curing me. And He reached out His hand and touched him, saying, I am willing; be cleansed by being cured. And instantly his leprosy was cured and cleansed.
—MATTHEW 8:2–3, AMP

But without faith it is impossible to please and be satisfactory to Him. For whoever would come near to God must [necessarily] believe that God exists and that He is the rewarder of those who earnestly and diligently seek Him [out].
—HEBREWS 11:6, AMP

He sends forth His Word and heals them and rescues them from the pit and destruction.
— PSALM 107:20, AMP

And Jesus, replying, said to them, have faith in God [constantly]. Truly I tell you, whoever says to this mountain, Be lifted up and thrown into the sea! and does not doubt at all in his heart but believes that what he says will take place, it will be done for him. For this reason I am telling you, whatever you ask for in prayer, believe (trust and be confident) that it is granted to you, and you will [get it].
—MARK 11:22–24, AMP

And these attesting signs will accompany those who believe: in My name they will drive out demons; they will speak in new languages; they will pick up serpents; and [even] if they drink anything deadly, it will not hurt them; they will lay their hands on the sick, and they will get well.
—MARK 16:17–18, AMP

So let us seize and hold fast and retain without wavering the hope we cherish and confess and our

Daily Living According to Scripture

acknowledgement of it, for He Who promised is reliable (sure) and faithful to His word.

—HEBREWS 10:23, AMP

Do not, therefore, fling away your fearless confidence, for it carries a great and glorious compensation of reward.

—HEBREWS 10:35, AMP

And this is the confidence (the assurance, the privilege of boldness) which we have in Him: [we are sure] that if we ask anything (make any request) according to His will (in agreement with His own plan), He listens to and hears us.

—1 JOHN 5:14, AMP

For God did not give us a spirit of timidity (of cowardice, of craven and cringing and fawning fear), but [He has given us a spirit] of power and of love and of calm and well-balanced mind and discipline and self-control.

—2 TIMOTHY 1:7, AMP

For though we walk (live) in the flesh, we are not carrying on our warfare according to the flesh and using mere human weapons. For the weapons of our warfare are not physical [weapons of flesh and blood], but they are mighty before God for the overthrow and destruction of strongholds, [Inasmuch as we] refute arguments and theories and reasonings and every proud and lofty thing that sets itself up against the [true] knowledge of God; and we lead every thought and purpose away captive into the obedience of Christ (the Messiah, the Anointed One).

—2 CORINTHIANS 10:3–5, AMP

I appeal to you therefore, brethren, and beg of you in view of [all] the mercies of God, to make a decisive dedication of your bodies [presenting all your members and faculties] as a living sacrifice, holy (devoted, concentrated) and well pleasing to God, which is your reasonable (rational, intelligent) service and spiritual worship. Do not be conformed to this world (this age), [fashioned after and adapted to its external, superficial customs], but be transformed (changed) by the [entire] renewal of your mind [by its new ideals and its new attitude], so that you may prove [for yourselves] what is the good and acceptable and perfect will of God, even the thing which is good and acceptable and perfect [in His sight for you].

—ROMANS 12:1–2, AMP

But you, beloved, build yourselves up [founded] on your most holy faith [make progress, rise like an edifice higher and higher], praying in the Holy Spirit.

—JUDE 20, AMP

Keep and guard your heart with all vigilance and above all that you guard, for out of it flow the springs of life.

—PROVERBS 4:23, AMP

Search me [thoroughly], O God, and know my heart! Try me and know my thoughts! And see if there is any wicked or hurtful way in me, and lead me in the way everlasting.

—PSALM 139:23–24, AMP

The heart is deceitful above all things, and it is exceedingly perverse and corrupt and severely, mortally sick! Who can know it [perceive, understand, be acquainted with his own heart and mind]? I the Lord search the mind, I try the heart, even to give to every man according to the fruit of his doings.

—JEREMIAH 17:9–10, AMP

Let the words of my mouth and the meditation of my heart be acceptable in Your sight, O Lord, my [firm, impenetrable] Rock and my Redeemer.

—PSALM 19:14, AMP

CHAPTER 5

Controlling Your Mind

E VERY DAY IN the United States doctors tell people that
they have a terminal disease. When I heard the word
terminal from my doctor, I felt a great cloud of darkness
attempt to envelop me. But darkness can only encroach
where there is no light. Darkness is the absence of light.
Satan, before he can gain control of any area of our lives,
must first remove the glorious light of Jesus Christ from
surrounding us.

Sickness in the body has a profound effect on a
person's spirit. Since the body has been designed by God
to express what is in the spirit of man, a sick body, already
at odds with the spirit because of the sin of Adam, wants
to revolt against any prompting of the spirit and focus all
attention on its weakness. The flesh wants every thought
to be on its treatment and care. The mind wants to go
along with the body because of its carnal nature, and the
two team up to overcome the influence of the spirit.
Darkness begins to set in because in the carnal mind, or
the physical man, there are no answers.

It is necessary that you understand that the enemy
wants to control your thinking, consume you with great
darkness and shut out all the light that the Holy Spirit

wants to shine on your condition. Beware of the following tactics of the enemy:

The enemy always wants you to regress, to go back or change, your spiritual pattern of pressing in to God.

He wants you to give up by painting a bleak picture in your mind. If you are going to succeed, the first thing that you must resolve in your mind is that you cannot allow thinking that tells you to go back or regress to a previous level of spirituality.

When you are battling sickness, there is sometimes an overwhelming temptation to sit around and regress into a pattern of thinking that tells you not to push yourself. I found that one of the keys to overcoming negative thinking patterns was to push myself to do things that my mind was telling me were too difficult for me to accomplish. When I was taking chemotherapy, I discovered that I could lie on the couch and feel bad, or I could be up doing something constructive and feel bad.

Pushing myself daily to do something constructive got me out of the environment of my own problems and into the realm of the promise of Luke 6:38 that assures us that if we will give, God will give unto us. I found that, by giving to others, God returned more to me than I could ever give.

Hebrews 11:1 tells us that "faith is the substance of things hoped for, the evidence of things not seen" (NKJV). Faith brings to us the reality of what we hope for. Hope is future, and faith is now. We must constantly have things that we hope for, such as overcoming physical infirmity, or else faith has no object to produce. Satan wants us to regress from hope and retreat into the hole of human reasoning.

Several times, during visits to the doctors who were treating me, the topic of medication for depression came up. It seemed that the doctors were worried about my mental well-being and wanted to help me by prescribing drugs to ease the mental load I was carrying. I had no desire to retreat or regress into some drug-induced utopia that would numb my abilities to deal with my situation from a spiritual perspective. I felt it imperative to press in to God further than I had ever been instead of regressing into false hope that the drugs would offer.

If you are going to be a person who is pleasing to God, you must diligently and earnestly seek Him. It pleases God when we diligently seek Him about our problems instead of retreating into some drug-induced state that renders us unable to feel anything emotionally or physically. Please keep in mind that I am referring to drugs for depression, not medicines that heal or drugs that alleviate physical suffering. Too many people, when they are battling sickness, retreat into the comfort that drugs offer; they lose their ability to hear what the Holy Spirit is trying to speak to them. You cannot regress; you must press in to God with all your heart.

If you think about regressing or going back, the enemy will present you with all kinds of opportunities to go back. You must constantly do things, dwell on things, and think on things that will cause hope to spring up within you.

The only power the enemy has over you is to get you to quit.

You must not allow sickness to overcome your spirit. The physical cannot overcome the spiritual. You must never lose sight of the fact that you are a spirit with a connection to this earth: your body. Never allow yourself to get to a place where you are more sensitive to the demands of the body than to the demands of the spirit.

Psalm 23 tells me that God will prepare a table before me

in the presence of my enemies. In your battle with sickness, God has a table that He will prepare for you that is loaded with everything you need. It may not necessarily have what you *want*, but it will always have what you *need*. Your sustenance from God is always ahead, never behind. I found that even in my darkest time, God would give me everything I needed if I would just go to the table He set before me and eat freely. If I would push aside the plate of self-pity and discouragement in which I wanted to indulge and instead consume His word of encouragement, I would be filled with the life that only His spirit could provide.

Never consume so much of the things of this present world that you lose you appetite for things of God. During times of sickness, avoid the temptation to look to the world to entertain and amuse you with its distractions. Those distractions might fill you up for a period of time, but they cannot sustain you. They will bring you nothing that will empower you to overcome. Only from the table of the Lord, the one He has prepared for you when all hell is raging against you, will you find food that is divinely empowered to enable you to overcome.

Never sit around and think about giving up, no matter how terrible the reports or how bad you feel. Constantly think on the things that will build your faith, and never lose the hope that you have within you.

The next phase of attack from Satan is suppression.

Inside every believer is the same spirit that raised Christ from the dead. It is God's design to give life to our mortal bodies. We also have the mind of Christ. Every believer has the potential to hear from God and have His life-altering power flow through our mortal beings. The enemy knows this and wants to suppress its flow.

If you open up your mind to the lies of the enemy, a

demonic bulldozer is released that begins to shove you in the direction that your thinking is going. If you are thinking about giving up, Satan comes in for the kill.

Coyote hunters have used a tactic for hunting that has proven quite effective. Since the coyote's habitat is stretched out over uninhabited areas, the hunter must do something to draw the coyote to him. Wily hunters use a recording of a wounded rabbit to entice the coyote to their trap. When the coyote hears the wounded rabbit's cry, he senses an easy dinner is nearby, and he comes in for the kill. It is the cry of the wounded rabbit that attracts the coyote.

I believe something very similar happens in the realm of the spirit. If you sit around and whine about your condition, if you let everyone know how terrible it is and constantly complain, you are sending out signals that you are wounded and hurt and in dire straits. I believe that there is nothing that attracts evil spirits like a person sending out messages in the spirit realm that he is wounded and in despair. It is then that the enemy reads your distress signals and comes in for the kill. Never allow the enemy to suppress the power of the Spirit of God that lives within you.

"He who dwells in the secret place of the Most High shall abide under the shadow of the Almighty," the psalmist declares (Psalm 91:1, NKJV). There is a place of safety under the shadow of God. As long as we are there, we are safe. Never allow the enemy to entice you to come out from under that covering. If you come out, you are fair game. No matter what you see with your natural senses, never come out from under the covering of God.

Suppress means "to take or put down by force." It also means, "to check or stop a natural flow." Suppressants are designed to stop something such as appetite, a cough, or pain. The enemy wants to stop or put a check on the natural flow. He will go after your desire to pray, worship and read the Word. If you open up your mind to the possibility of giving in to sickness, suppression of the spiritual flow of God to combat the negative mental process will stop the life-giving power to sustain you in the battle. Your strength will leave, and you will face your greatest enemy, not in the power of the Spirit, but in the power of your own strength. You are no match with your limited power for the onslaught that you will encounter.

It is here that the enemy might begin to harass you about your commitment to God and tell you that you have served Him in vain. Thoughts may invade your thinking that question why sickness is happening to someone who has tried to serve God faithfully and lived as well as they knew how. As the old proverb tells us, "We cannot keep the birds from circling overhead, but we can keep them from building a nest in our hair," so we must never allow that kind of thinking to take root in our lives. We must take a firm stand and never allow ourselves to be moved from our position of faith in the integrity of God.

Suppressants are designed to stop or control some-thing. They *have no power to cure* the condition. If you have a cough and go to the drugstore to buy cough syrup, you are purchasing something that will keep you from coughing, but it will not *cure* your cough.

One of the main reasons that I chose not to take med-ication for depression is because the medication acts only as a suppressant. The medication would only *suppress* the symptoms of the depression, not *cure* them. If you have fear, anxiety or worry during a bout with sickness, would it not be much better to feast on the Word of God that will cure the symptoms than to take a pill that would only suppress them?

Drugs are one of the major avenues that can open a person for demonic influence. Drugs overwhelm the phys-ical and mental aspects of your personality and keep them from expressing whatever is controlling you. If you are full of fear and anxiety about your condition, the doctor can prescribe a drug that will render your body incapable of expressing the symptom. All the medication does is to suppress the problem, not cure it. Nothing has changed but the fact that the drug is more powerful than whatever symptoms are bothering you.

Medication for depression when you are battling physical infirmities can render you ineffective to wage a spiritual war against the problem. It has the potential to affect your ability to pray, hear from God, and most of all, snuff out your drive to push yourself into the realm of the Spirit. You have a problem, but taking something to suppress it will never get you out of the problem. Anti-depressants will simply allow the problems to remain without the ability to manifest themselves.

If you are battling depression, there is a reason, but problems need to be revealed for what they are in our lives. I hated what depression was doing to me to the degree that I was willing to do whatever was necessary to overcome it. For me, evening sessions of prayer in the sanctuary of the church was the only way I could keep my mind from going ballistic. It would have been easier to take a pill, but I found that pleading my case before God and allowing the Holy Spirit to strengthen me sustained me. This spiritual life-flow is the very thing that the enemy wants to suppress in your life. You must do everything you can to keep it flowing. I felt that, for me, prayer, not pills, would keep the source of life flowing.

We must believe that either the God whom we serve can keep and sustain us, or we need to sell out to the world and its dictates. A deadly combination of the two will never work. God wants to keep us at a place where we can pray our way through things, not sit as a zombie under the influence of something that renders us ineffective to fight the good fight of faith.

If the enemy is going to have any influence or control over you, he must first depress the Holy Spirit's ability to transmit the life of God to you.

Depress means, "to cast down or put under." If the presence of the Spirit of God is cast down and put under, we are left with nothing but our own carnal thinking to guide us.

Looking at sickness from the perspective of doctors' reports and physical feelings is usually beyond the natural mind's ability to overcome. Taking the available data about your sickness and analyzing it from every possible perspective, the natural mind becomes overloaded as it tries to deal with all the multiplied possibilities and will usually resort to the negative. You begin to think about the negative and dwell on the negative, and finally, you become negative.

The Scriptures tell us, "as a man thinks in his spirit so he becomes." (See Proverbs 23:7.) Your life is a mirror of your thinking. If your thinking is under the influence of the natural mind, then your spirit, which is your connection to God, is buried under the power of that negative thinking. Your natural mind is shouting at you louder than the gentle promptings of the Spirit. The more negative your thinking becomes, the more depressed your spirit becomes. Instead of being governed by the mind of Christ, you will be governed by human reasoning, which has no real or lasting solutions.

One of my favorite accounts in the Bible is that of David and his near-disaster in the city of Ziklag. (See 1 Samuel 30.) David, who has been anointed King of Israel, is biding his time until God's dealings with Israel and King Saul are completed. David is very much in the will of God and is undergoing a preparation that will culminate with his leading the nation of Israel into the most glorious time that nation will ever enjoy.

Upon returning to their hideaway in Ziklag, David and his men discover that their enemies have ravaged the city, burned their dwellings, stolen their possessions and kidnapped their families. The men are distraught and completely overwhelmed by what their natural understanding is telling them. They are so angry that they look to David and blame him for the whole mess. They begin to plot among themselves to stone David and secure new leadership.

David, however, does a remarkable thing. He removes himself from the chaos and seeks the face of God. The Bible says that he encouraged himself in God. As he communed with God, he was given supernatural revelation as to what he should do and what the outcome of his obedience would be. God told David to pursue his enemies and that he would recover all that was lost. David did as God commanded, and everything that God had spoken to him became a reality.

In times of sickness, we must constantly encourage ourselves in God. In the darkest of circumstances, when in the natural understanding everything seems lost, God can give us a sense of direction that will bring into existence the very thing that our natural mind tells us can never happen. It is imperative that you never allow depression to take root in your life. Your life-giving source, the Holy Spirit, must have the liberty to communicate to your mind what truth is. Romans 12 tells us that we are not to be conformed to this world, but rather be transformed by the renewing of our mind. In other words, the only transformation you can experience is when your mind, with its natural reasoning, is renewed and under the dominion of the Holy Spirit. Your outlook will change, your countenance will be different, and your faith will sustain you during your toughest battles.

During times of sickness, we must learn to play the hand we have been dealt. There are certain realities that you must deal with, and wishing they would go away is not a realistic option. Resenting your situation will rob you of day-to-day little things that make up your life. Resentment will steal from your relationship with family and friends, which leaves you with only your carnal mind dwelling on how unfair your circumstances are.

If you are going to overcome the death grip in which sickness wants to ensnare you, you must come to the conclusion that there are certain realities that you must deal with and not allow yourself to drift off into some mental nirvana that just wishes it would all go away. You must survey the situation and devise a battle plan. You must understand that depression is an enemy of wholeness. Recognize the avenue that leads to depression and take whatever detours are necessary to avoid it.

Another death grip sickness brings is obsession.

It is easy to become obsessed with your dilemma and shut down all other aspects of life and concentrate exclusively on your own needs, but life is in giving. If you shut down your giving, you will cut off the flow of life to yourself. Even when you are sick, life goes on. As much as you possibly can, determine to be a giver. Giving will take your mind off yourself and your needs and will bring a degree of joy to your life as you bless others in your own time of battle.

Being obsessed with yourself shuts you off from everyone and everything around you. If you focus on yourself, your resources consist only of what your strength can bring to the situation. If you choose to give, you will find that God will give back to you in direct proportion to the measure in which you give to others.

Controlling Your Mind

Life flows back to you as you give to others. Never get to the point that the world revolves around you and your sickness. Determine to bless others when you are around them. Always give them more than they give to you. Obsession with sickness will choke out many avenues of blessings that God wants to send your way.

An *oppressor* is one who rules by putting down all opposition by force. An oppressor wants to remove anything other than himself as the channel of life. Freedom to hear from any other source, freedom to express any other thoughts, and freedom to move from venue to venue for life-sustaining power are denied. Only what the oppressor wants you to hear, feel and experience are allowed. The enemy wants to oppress you to the degree that he controls what you think, what you listen to and what you see. He wants to oppress all sources of life to you. He wants to flood you with lies and bury your spirit under a layer of unholy silt that renders you unable to hear from God.

Never allow the enemy any place in your life. You cannot allow anger, resentment, or a *Why me?* attitude to get a foothold in your life. These attitudes become landing strips for the enemy to launch his attacks on your mind. He will use these tactics to oppress everything that will bring you encouragement and help. Constantly be on alert for anything that will reduce your focus and sphere of influence. Keep your channels open, and God will sustain you during any battle.

CHAPTER 6

There Is Hope Again

I entered IUPUI Medical Center in early April of 1996, full of apprehension and a gnawing sense of dread about my first chemo treatment. Over and over again I thought, *What will it feel like when this stuff enters my body? Will it hurt? Will I become instantly nauseated? When will my hair fall out? Will I lose feeling in my feet?*

None of these concerns were alleviated when the nurses came in to start the IV. There is no way to put into words the feelings that flood you when you take your first chemo treatment. Wearing protective gloves, the nurses carried the drugs into the room. On the container was the same "Danger: Hazardous Material" warning you see on semi-trucks carrying hazardous materials down the interstate. *Whoa,* I thought, *if the nurses are this concerned about getting a drop of this stuff on them, what is a whole bag of it going to do to my insides?* Seeing a container with a blue label with skull and crossbones did not increase my comfort level about what was going to flow into my bloodstream.

When the IV drip started, I kept waiting for the effects to hit me with some sort of powerful force. I waited, and waited and waited, yet nothing negative happened. After the first hour of receiving treatment and being able to endure it, I breathed a sigh of relief. I learned on that first day of treatment, the best way to get through it is to relax, take a nap and sleep through as much of it as you possibly can, and not allow fear and agitating thoughts to steal your strength and clutter your mind.

At the end of the first week of treatment, I developed flu-like symptoms that intensified after every session. I was nauseated, had no desire to eat, ached in all my joints, and had numbness in both feet. My strength was slowly depleted, allowing me to do only simple tasks, such as pushing the grocery cart through Wal-Mart. I found that if I over-extended myself, my body did not have the ability to bounce back. Strength became precious and had to be rationed at the proper times. I had to find the stamina to minister. I stole strength from other, less worthwhile activities and saved it for those times that were the most important to me: Sundays and Wednesdays.

Though I have been afflicted since my early twenties with male pattern baldness, I am very attached to what hair I have, and during most of my adult years, I have worn a full beard. The day my hair fell out, as any chemo patient will tell you, initiated me into a club I never wanted to join: *The Club of the Seriously Sick*. After the hair loss, it was hard to hide my condition from all the casual observers. The disease that was hidden inside me was now on display for everyone to observe and judge.

It happened so fast. On Monday there was not a hint of what was about to happen, but on Tuesday, it was like a switch was flipped, and my hair just let loose. To my horror, after scratching my beard, my hand was full of hair. I took my hand and dusted my beard right off my face. I rubbed my fingers across my head, and they, too, became covered with hair.

I had dreaded this experience from the first day of

chemo, but hair loss was just one of the many humbling experiences that a bout with cancer would bring. Wanting to end the process as rapidly as I could, I called my barber, drove twenty miles to his shop, and yielded to his shears.

My physical appearance was so drastically altered that many of my friends and acquaintances no longer recognized me. I had trouble dealing with the new person the mirror was reflecting. Many of the distinguishing features that make me the unique character I am, such as hair, beard, eyebrows and eyelashes had vanished. Replacing my normal reflection was a bizarre hybrid of Mr. Clean and Uncle Fester. The new guy in the mirror took some time to adjust to.

The first Sunday service after the hair loss was particularly difficult. Still struggling with my new looks, I hid behind the piano and directed the worship leader to conduct the service until it was time for me to deliver the morning message. Several members of our congregation, seeing the shiny domed preacher sitting in my place, assumed I was gone and that he was a guest speaker. When my distinct voice revealed the identity of their supposed guest speaker, several people literally jumped in their seats. Though it was somewhat amusing, I had a tough time getting past the looks on people's faces as I delivered the morning message.

The physical effects of chemotherapy humbled me and served as a constant reminder of the disease residing within me. I would be pushing a cart through Wal-Mart, mulling over the grocery list, when a stare from a child, observing my pale and hairless features, jolted me back to the reality that I had cancer. My collection of baseball hats became prized possessions. I would not leave the house without a hat, and if my wife had not put up such a squawk, I would have preached on Sunday morning wearing a hat to match my jogging suit.

Despite the hardships chemotherapy brings, the resiliency of the human spirit can triumph over all the adversity and side effects of the standard cancer-fighting treatment. I learned to adapt to the new image in the mirror, and I learned to return a smile when encountered with a stare. I would go on the offensive during conversations with people who wanted to know but were afraid to ask. I learned to adapt to the physical weakness I experienced and to conserve energy for the things that were worthwhile. I loved golf, and I was determined that the effects of chemo were not going to rob me of one of the things I enjoyed most. I would go to the course, play as many holes as my strength would allow, then return home and rest. I loved to preach. I would go to church, give the congregation everything I had, and go home and rest.

Chemotherapy taught me to conserve strength and only use my resources for worthwhile things. One of the biggest problems I see in the church today is that God's people expend all their resources, both natural and spiritual, on things that in the scope of eternity matter little. The apostle Paul, writing to the church at Ephesus, tells us to "not be drunk with wine, in which is dissipation, but be filled with the Spirit" (see Ephesians 5:18, NKJV).

Many well-meaning believers spend all their strength on worldly endeavors and have very little to give to God. They are too tired to pray, read the Word or go to church. They are unable to deposit anything godly into the lives of those seeking God because they have become spiritually bankrupt. I learned a powerful principle during chemo that has become a cornerstone of my existence: You must conserve your energy, emotionally, physically, and spiritually for those things that matter the most.

THERE ARE SOME THINGS
YOU JUST CANNOT EXPLAIN

I was convinced that the chemo was not going to have any impact on the tumors in my bladder and felt very strongly that the upcoming reevaluation would confirm my diagnosis. I had yielded to the pleas of friends and family, taken the two treatments, and was now prepared to hear Dr. Rowland compassionately tell me that we had fought a valiant fight, but my medical options were over. At least it was comforting to think that there would be no more hospitals, chemo needles and hospital food. I was either going to get a miracle or die.

When you have been diagnosed with a potentially deadly condition, you build a wall around your emotions to insulate you from the detrimental effects of bad news. You learn to hear the negative reports, but not to allow them to bring your emotions to the surface. The initial negative diagnosis literally flattens you. It is bigger than your ability to deal with it, and it produces a storm of emotions that tosses you helplessly through the winds it created in your soul. Stunned with the reality of that initial experience, you determine to never allow yourself to get caught in another emotional firestorm, so you build a wall around your emotions to contain them. You become determined to look adversity in the eye and not blink.

Our drive to Indianapolis that June morning was devoid of conversation and emotional exchanges. I was going to endure the cystoscope, hear the bad news, thank the medical staff for their efforts and bid a fond farewell to IUPUI. Nothing anyone could say or do was going to get me emotionally involved.

Because of the location of my tumors, I had become all too familiar with having a cystoscope inserted into my urinary tract. It is a humbling experience to lie unclad on a gurney, while someone I hardly knew examined my most private areas. The procedure lasts from three to five minutes. I learned to relax, cooperate with the physician and force my mind to dwell on a more pleasant topic.

After a few pleasantries, I hopped on the table, adjusted my thinking, and waited for the local anesthetic to kick in. *In three minutes, it will be over with,* I thought, *and I will never have to do this again.*

As the procedure started, I awaited the usual small talk the doctor used to divert my attention away from the discomfort the cystoscope produces. I could sense an intensity of examination that superseded his prior look to determine the size of the tumors. His silence confirmed my suspicions that the chemo had failed, the tumors had grown, and my prognosis was headed farther south.

The words that came from behind the sheet that separated visual contact will forever be etched in my memory. "You have had a remarkable response to the chemo, a dramatic, near miracle-type of reaction to the regimen of drugs you have taken," the doctor cheerfully reported. "The tumors are completely gone, and I cannot even find any evidence of where they were." But the same wall I had built around my emotions to keep the negative ones from overflowing kept the positive ones in check as well.

While the urologist was slapping me on the shoulder about my good fortune, congratulating me like someone who had just hit the game-winning home run in the seventh game of the World Series, I lay emotionless, unable to respond to the greatest medical report of my life.

While I lay in stunned silence for what seemed an eternity, trying desperately to muster up faith enough to believe that I was actually in the realm of reality, a flurry of activity electrified the atmosphere in the examining room.

The oncologist had arrived, carrying with him results of prior examinations and was busily comparing them with the test I had just undergone. As I strained to hear their medical chitchat and get a layman's grasp on their terminology, one word kept coming out that I didn't need a medical dictionary to understand: *cure*.

After their mini-medical conference, both doctors sat down beside me and explained that the three golf-ball-sized tumors in my bladder were no longer there. In their medical opinion, I had had a dramatic response to the two sessions of chemotherapy, or in baseball terms *I had hit a grand slam on a 0-2 count with two outs in the bottom of the ninth*.

As I listened to the doctors talking, the words *remarkable, dramatic* and *near miracle* kept coming up as well. Both doctors wanted me to take the last four chemotherapy treatments and have another evaluation in three months. If everything remained the same, they wanted me to have the originally scheduled surgery. Both doctors seemed delighted to tell me that my odds had greatly improved, and there was now a strong possibility of a cure.

As I left the examination room to relay the news to Ronda, a spring of pent-up emotions began to seep through the wall I had built to protect myself from all the bad medical news of the past five months. I simply could not express, with proper emotions, the way I was feeling inside. I delivered the best news Ronda had heard in the past few months with the countenance of a man about to plan his funeral.

I wanted to shout out the good news, but my body would not let me. It would literally be days before my physical countenance would be able to express the joy that was rising up from my spirit. Ronda, absolutely caught off guard by the wonderful news, burst into tears and danced a little jig in the waiting room, rejoicing in the miracle that

God had dropped into our laps.

Our conversation on the way home included a topic we had not been able to talk about: the future. Even though that day had brought us new hope, there were still the four treatments of chemotherapy, a major surgery, and an extended hospital stay and recovery ahead of us.

If there was one thing this ordeal had taught us, it was to live one day at a time. I knew that the doctors were giving credit to the chemotherapy, but on the drive to Laconia that day, I felt an absolute assurance that God Almighty had touched me in a powerful way and that He had a plan for my future. The prayers of the saints and the power of faith had prevailed mightily against the cancer that was trying to take my life. In the coming months, it would be confirmed to me in a stunning revelation of what percentage medicine had played in my actual recovery.

CHAPTER 7

How to Find a Relationship With God in the Midst of Your Problems

THERE IS A strong possibility that the reason you are reading this book is because you are struggling with a physical infirmity. You may have just been diagnosed and are looking for a game plan to counterattack what is coming at you, or you may be in the last stages of cancer and desperately need a miracle. You may be a person of great faith, or someone who is reading this book because a well-meaning friend or relative thrust it into your lap. The reason you are reading this account could be any one of a hundred reasons, but there is a good chance that you find yourself in the middle of something you cannot wish away, pray away, rebuke away or cast away. Up until this point, it just will not go away, so you have to deal with it.

God is not the author of sickness. It is the enemy who has come to kill, steal and destroy. Jesus became flesh to destroy the works of the devil. (See 1 John 3:8.) Every evil thing on this planet, whether sickness, hurricanes, tornadoes or any natural disaster, is a result of Adam's sin and his forfeiture of dominion to Satan. He rules this natural world for a season, but God has empowered us through His Spirit to overcome this world, our sinful flesh and the devil. We must understand James' admonition in the Bible to "submit yourselves...to God. Resist the devil, and he will flee from you" (James 4:7, KJV). God is not the creator of your problem, nor did He have any hand in causing it. In fact, just the opposite is true; He desperately wants to help you overcome it.

If you have never had a born-again experience that comes through faith in God's grace, your spiritual condition is far worse than any disease you may be battling. You must understand that our physical condition is only temporary, but our spiritual condition is eternal. The born-again believer is assured that though the outer man is progressively decaying and wasting away, his inner self is being progressively renewed day after day. (See 2 Corinthians 4:16.) The very Spirit that raised Jesus from the dead dwells in the life of a believer, and He has the power to give that same kind of spiritual life to his mortal body. (See Romans 8:11.)

It is easy when you desperately need a miracle to go after the hand of God instead of His face. You have a life-threatening dilemma, and you want God to take care of it. You may have scanned the bookshelves and airwaves trying to find the "How to" word on how to get God to move on your behalf, but you may not have realized that God is a God of relationships, not programs. If you are outside Christ and after a miracle, file this in your memory bank. If somehow you escape death this time, you are only prolonging the inevitable. "...It is appointed for men to die once, but after this the judgment" (Hebrews 9:27, NKJV). If you are lost, you need more than a miracle; *you need salvation.*

All of us must "seek first the kingdom of God and His righteousness, and all these things shall be added to you" (Matthew 6:33, NKJV). All of us must have a residence change from the domain of darkness to the kingdom of

His marvelous light.

Everyone on this planet needs a savior, and genuine salvation cannot be attained by any other means except through Jesus. Many people feel that they are people of faith, but the object of their faith is not what Jesus did for them; the object of their faith is in their own ability to be good. The Bible explicitly informs us that the path to eternal destruction is broad and many are on it, but the path to heaven is narrow and few are on it. (See Matthew 7:13–14.) Contrary to this scriptural fact, the vast majority of Americans, according to Gallup polls, believe they are going to heaven. Why the contradiction?

Most people in America feel that though they may have a few flaws, they are basically pretty good people. Many believe that one day, they will stand before God and watch as the angels place all their good deeds on one side of the scales and all their bad deeds on the other side of the scales. They feel pretty confident that the good they do will outweigh the bad, and their entrance to Heaven will be a lock. They look around at all their friends, compare themselves to them, and come out looking all right. Many in America do not feel the need for a savior because they are confident that their goodness will get them into Heaven.

The Law of God is a reflection of His nature. It reveals to man what God expects man to be. But the Law of God has one serious flaw: our inability to live it. Many erroneously think God gave us the law to guide us along the way; obeying it the best we can, living it by our own strength, and then having a whimsical Heavenly Father allowing us into Heaven because we put in a good effort.

Romans 3:19–24 gives us the following description of our relationship to the Law:

> Now we know that whatever the Law says, it speaks to those who are under the Law, so that [the murmurs and

excuses of] every mouth may be hushed and all the world may be held accountable to God. For no person will be justified (made righteous, acquitted, and judged acceptable) in His sight by observing the works prescribed by the Law. For [the real function of] the Law is to make men recognize and be conscious of sin [not mere perception, but an acquaintance with sin which works toward repentance, faith and holy character]. But now the righteousness of God has been revealed independently and altogether apart from the Law, although actually it is attested by the Law and the Prophets. Namely, the righteousness of God which comes by believing with personal trust and confident reliance on Jesus Christ (the Messiah). [And it is meant] for all who believe. For there is no distinction. Since all have sinned and are falling short of the honor and glory which God bestows and receives. [All] are justified and made upright and in right standing with God, freely and gratuitously by His grace (His unmerited favor and mercy) through the redemption which is [provided] in Christ Jesus. (AMP)

Every living being on this planet shares this common trait: an inability to measure up to the standards of God. The law was given to us to drive home that very point. My sin, your sin—anybody's sin—does one thing: It separates us from God. We cannot be reconciled to God by our misguided attempts to placate God through our own efforts to be as good as possible. God's Word stands firm. If I violate one ordinance, I have violated the entire code. One sin separates me from God.

You and I must see ourselves as a violator of the Law of God and in desperate need of a savior—someone who can do for us that which we cannot do for ourselves. That someone, that savior, is Jesus. Jesus left the portals of glory, donned an earthly suit, and through His relationship with the Father came to earth and lived a sinless life on my behalf, because I could not do it.

Everything Jesus did on earth, He did on my behalf. He overcame sin through His connection to His Father's empowering ability while being fully human. Though He was tempted as we are today, He never yielded to temptation's pull. He overcame the god of this world, His humanity and the positions of fame that many wanted to bestow upon Him. He came with a purpose, and nothing could stop Him because the motivation that drove Him was His great concern for our condition: *separation from God because of our inability to keep the Law of God.*

Not only did Jesus do some things for us that we could not do, but He also made Himself responsible for our sinful condition. He reversed our spiritual condition through His death, burial and resurrection. Second Corinthians 5:19 tells us that "it was God [personally present] in Christ, reconciling and restoring the world to favor with Himself, not counting up and holding against [men] their trespasses [but canceling them], and committing to us the message of reconciliation (of the restoration to favor)" (AMP).

The God of this universe loves us to the degree that He made Himself responsible for our spiritual condition in Adam, and He reversed it in Christ. The simple point I am making is that we "all have sinned and fall short of the glory of God" (Romans 3:23, NKJV) and that sin has separated us from God. God gave man the Law to reveal to him his condition. Each of us must see that, in our present condition, we cannot keep God's Holy Law. The soul that sins shall die, according to the Bible, and that leaves each of us in a spiritual quandary, desiring favor with God but unable to attain it through our goodness. The Law was given to hush our mouths concerning our goodness and to lead us to the only good, true One, Jesus. What you and I will never be able to do because of the weakness of our flesh *Jesus did.*

Jesus kept the Law of God perfectly, and He did it not to impress God, but for my behalf because I could not do it.

Jesus' mission did not end after He had lived a sinless life; He took that sinless life to a cross and became sin on my behalf. Second Corinthians 5:21 explains it this way: "For our sake He made Christ [virtually] to be sin Who knew no sin, so that in and through Him we might become [endued with, viewed as being in, and examples of] the righteousness of God [what we ought to be, approved and acceptable and in right relationship with Him, by His goodness] (AMP).

Jesus took upon Himself my sin and made Himself responsible for what I had done wrong. He became my sin and died because of my inability to keep the Law of God. My inability put Him on the cross, and His love for me kept Him there. His death two thousand years ago was really my death. He took upon Himself my spiritual condition and died with it. The apostle Paul, writing to the Colossians, gives us this powerful revelation:

> And although you at one time were estranged and alienated from Him and were of hostile attitude of mind in your wicked activities; Yet now has [Christ, the Messiah] reconciled [you to God] in the body of His flesh through death, in order to present you holy and faultless and irreproachable in His [the Father's] presence."
>
> —COLOSSIANS 1:21–22 (AMP)

He continues by saying:

> And you who were dead in trespasses and in the uncircumcision of your own flesh (your sensuality, your sinful carnal nature), [God] brought to life together with [Christ] having freely forgiven us all our transgression, having cancelled and blotted out and wiped away the handwriting of the note (bond) with its legal

85

decrees and demands which was in force and stood against us (hostile to us). This [note with its regulations, decrees, and demands] He set aside and cleared completely out of our way by nailing it to [His] cross.
—COLOSSIANS 2:13–14 (AMP)

Jesus' death completely satisfied the legal system of God. Jesus died on my behalf. The punishment that I deserved because of my sin, Jesus took upon Himself. Isaiah, the Old Testament prophet who lived hundreds of years before Jesus' birth, prophesied what Jesus would do one day for every living man, woman and child. Isaiah proclaimed:

Surely, He has born our griefs (sicknesses, weaknesses, and distresses) and carried our sorrows and pains [of punishment], yet we [ignorantly] considered Him stricken, smitten, and afflicted by God [as if with leprosy]. But He was wounded for our transgressions, He was bruised for our guilt and iniquities; the chastisement [needful to obtain] peace and well-being for us was upon Him, and with the stripes [that wounded] Him we are healed and made whole. All we like sheep have gone astray, we have turned every one to his own way; and the Lord has made to light upon Him the guilt and iniquity of us all.
—ISAIAH 53:4–6 (AMP)

Although it is a spiritual and historical fact that Jesus died, He did not stay dead very long. Once the regulations and requirements under the legal system of God had been satisfied, Jesus had the very first born-again experience. Jesus, dead with my death, having become the propitiation for my sin, or that which appeased God, was raised from the dead by the power of the Almighty God. His resurrection actually was my resurrection as well. He was the first person to die and not be overcome by death. God raised Him from the dead on my behalf. Jesus was the firstborn of many brethren. (See Hebrews 2:11.) His born-again experience would be the first of millions that would follow, as the gospel, the good news of Jesus, was proclaimed around the world.

The Bible proclaims that the very same Spirit that raised Jesus from the dead lives in the life of the believer, and it will quicken itself in us and give life to our mortal bodies.

It is the grace and kindness of God that should lead us to repentance and saving faith in Jesus. It is God's great love for us that is displayed in His grace, epitomized by the things Jesus did for us. His grace is that part of His nature that allows Him to have quality relationships with broken humanity. Grace is wonderful, but it is only one side of the story. God's grace has been extended to every man, but not every man will cash in on the great benefits of God's plan of salvation of man.

Faith is your grip on God. "Without faith it is impossible to please Him" (Hebrews 11:6, NKJV). God wants man to believe Him at His word. During His earthly ministry, Jesus constantly emphasized the fact that man *must* believe. I am not talking about an intellectual acknowledgment that Jesus is the Son of God. The demons believe that and shudder at the thought. I am talking about a faith that will connect you to God. "Faith is the substance of the things hoped for, the evidence of things not seen" (Hebrews 11:1, NKJV). You must believe for yourself that God actually did all these things on your behalf. You must believe that everything Jesus did was done on your behalf. You must believe that He was your substitute. You must believe that He lived a sinless life for you, died your death, was buried with your burial and was resurrected with your resurrection.

Ephesians 2:8–9 says it this way: "For it is by free grace (God's unmerited favor) that you are saved (delivered from judgment and made partakers of Christ's salvation) through

[your] faith. And this [salvation] is not of yourselves [of your own doing, it came not through your own striving], but it is the gift of God. Not because of works [not the fulfillment of the Law's demands], lest any man should boast [It is not the result of what anyone can possibly do, so no one can pride himself in it or take glory to himself.]" (AMP).

None of these marvelous things came as a result of anything you have ever done or ever will do. They come to us because of God's marvelous grace. Your faith in these facts will release to you the marvelous benefits of grace, peace with God, and an eternal salvation that will never fade away.

If you are reading this book and have never established a relationship with God through the atoning work of Jesus, I have good news and glad tidings of great joy for you. Though your outer man might be decaying and battling sickness, the same Spirit that raised Jesus from the dead can come into you, quicken itself in you, and give life to your mortal body. Through your faith in His awesome grace, you can ask the Holy Spirit to come into your life, destroy the old man of sin, and birth a new man full of the presence of God. You can have the same born-again experience that Jesus had when God raised Him from the dead.

Pray this simple prayer with faith, and a miracle will transpire.

> *Dear Lord God, I believe and have simple faith that I have sinned and have separated myself from all that You are. I now realize that I need a savior. I need someone to do for me what I cannot do for myself. I believe that You lived a sinless life on my behalf. I believe that You took my sin upon Yourself and died my death on the cross of Calvary. I believe You were buried with my burial and were raised with my resurrection. I have faith that if I will*

*believe in my heart and confess with my mouth
these great provisions of grace that I will be saved.
Thank You, Jesus, for Your great love for me. I am
now asking for Your Spirit to come and dwell in me
and give me life. I, by faith, believe that the same
Spirit that raised Jesus from the dead now lives in
me. Thank You for this great salvation that is found
only in the name of Jesus.*

If you prayed that prayer with faith, you are now a
member of the household of God. You have peace with
God, as well as the mind of Christ. Your spiritual condition is much more important than your physical condition.
One of the main reasons for this little deviation from my
story is that I wanted to tell you that, although doctors and
the medical field were of some help to me during my
ordeal, it was only through my relationship with Jesus that
I was able to overcome. And I want every reader of this
book to have an opportunity to experience the same
power of relationship with Jesus that sustained me during
my battle with cancer.

CHAPTER 8

Conforming Me
to His Image

DESPITE THE DISAPPEARANCE of the tumors in my bladder, both the urologist and the oncologist insisted that I continue the regimen of prescribed chemotherapy. The idea of enduring four more five-day stays in the hospital and taking drugs that ravaged my body was almost more than I could bear. Even though I could see some light at the end of the tunnel, I desperately wanted that chapter in my life to end as soon as possible.

The biggest motivational ploy the doctors used to get me to continue the treatments was the promised removal of the urostomy urinary diversion system they had constructed to do the work of my ailing bladder. To accommodate the urostomy device, I had to wear pants at least one size too large, suspenders and oversized shirts. The constant care, restrictions on certain activities and sleeping problems it caused sometimes drove me past my spiritual parameters into fits of anger accompanied by rivers of tears. There were times that I absolutely despised the restrictions it imposed on my lifestyle and the embarrassment it caused. With the goal of the removal of the urostomy as my motivation, I gave myself over to the chemo treatments.

The doctors were fairly confident that after the chemo

treatments, followed by a three-month recuperation period, I would be able to have the originally intended surgery and have the urostomy removed. I found myself in a Catch-22 situation. I wanted them to reconnect my now cancer-free bladder and go about business as normal, but in their vast medical experience, my greatest chance of long-term survival was to have my bladder removed and replaced with one they would construct from parts of my colon.

Even though I pleaded with them, it was going to be their way or not at all. The surgeon told me, in no uncertain terms, that he would not reconnect my bladder. He assured me that I would not be able to find a surgeon that would. By this stage of the game, I was ready to do anything to get rid of that appliance attached to my side.

The rules had been defined, and I reluctantly agreed to them. After the chemo regimen ended, I would give my body some time to renew its strength and undergo surgery to have my bladder removed, as well as the urostomy. I would live out my days with a bladder constructed of a borrowed reflux valve and a three-inch section from both my large and small intestine.

During those last four chemo treatments, I learned a great deal about endurance. I was confident that the things I was hoping for would be realized if I could just endure the process. Spiritually, the Word of God tells us, "he who endures to the end will be saved" (Matthew 24:13, NKJV). Anyone who has ever tried to walk with God knows that our faith is only the substance of the things we hope for. Hope keeps us in the game, while faith brings us the substance, or reality, for what we believe.

Many times in our lives we do not want to have to endure *anything*. We fail to see that pressing on in difficult times builds endurance in our lives. Without endurance we cannot possibly finish the purposes God has for our lives.

We must know with certainty that God takes no delight in believers who shrink back in difficulty or lie down and quit. (See Hebrews 10:34.)

I understand fully that the outcome of my faith is the salvation of my soul. If I will fully submit myself to the process that God is allowing in my life, I will develop enough endurance to overcome every obstacle that this world can throw at me. So many times we want out of the trial before it has accomplished its purpose. "God causes all things to work together for good to those who love God, to those who are called according to His purpose" (Romans 8:28, NIV).

Trials lose their power over us when we submit to the purposes behind them. Trials test our faith. Scriptures admonish us to rejoice when trials come because they reveal the depth of our spirituality. (See James 1:2–4.) When we are squeezed during difficult times in our lives, the quality of the fruit that resides within us, either good or bad, is exposed. Trials, in essence, are tests orchestrated by God to reveal to the believer the reality of their spiritual maturity. We never fail God's tests. We simply take them over and over and over, or until we finally pass. During the last four chemotherapy treatments, I took the same spiritual test several times.

In the early stages of the chemo treatments, I simply wanted it to be over. I was weary of the ordeal, had little desire to learn any new spiritual insights, and was conscious of only my own dilemma. I despised what was happening and was literally blind to what was going on around me. Without realizing it, I had become so caught up in my own misery that I was losing compassion for those who were in similar situations. Instead of reaching out to others, I withdrew into a shell on Monday and emerged on Friday in time to go home without doing anything productive for anyone during the week.

Before every chemo treatment, I had to have blood tests to determine if I was strong enough to endure that week's treatment. After the blood was drawn, I was escorted to a room to await the results. Everything I ever wanted to know about what cancer was really like but was afraid to ask could have been answered by simply looking at the people sitting around me. There were little hairless children in wheelchairs too young to even comprehend what was happening to them, accompanied by parents desperately trying to keep on their game faces. Pale teenagers wearing various types of caps and scarves in a vain attempt to hide their disease waited patiently, hoping to hear even the slightest hint of good news. The elderly, many wearing surgical masks, often in wheelchairs, sat quietly awaiting word if their frail conditions would prohibit them from receiving another life-stretching treatment. In that room you could see the beginning stages of cancer all the way to its end result.

To fulfill the commission of Jesus, we have to be touched with the feelings of the infirmities of others. During those visits to that waiting room, I was forced to deal with the reality that, for most of my life as a healthy pastor, I had little compassion for the sick. Suddenly, I was a part of that world. Although God is not the author of sickness, He was using the trial I was going through to conform me to His image. He became the faithful High Priest because He experienced the human condition. He is able to sympathize with our weakness and problems because He lived the human experience. When I come into the presence of Jesus, I am coming to someone who understands.

Suddenly, I understood sickness. Suddenly, I understood what it was like to have cancer. Suddenly, I understood the mental, physical and spiritual battles that cancer patients face. It was no longer theory, but some-thing God had worked out in my life that I was to use for the benefit of those who were going to come behind me, fighting the same battle that I was going through.

When I submitted to the trials, I began to receive reve-lation from the Holy Spirit that changed my life forever. The Scriptures counsel us to submit to God, resist the devil, and he will flee from us. Submission to my trial opened up a door of relationship with God that I had never experi-enced and literally caused the enemy to withdraw from the situation, taking with him all his lies, accusations and fears. Those last four chemo treatments became a spiritual training ground that has completely altered the way I approach those who are fighting physical infirmities.

In December 1996, after completing the regimen of chemo and allowing my body three months to regain its strength, I underwent surgery at IUPUI to have my bladder and prostate removed and replaced with a continent urinary diversion device. Dr. Randall Rowland performed the suc-cessful surgery, and after an eleven-day stay in the hospital, I was released to carry on with life.

In spite of a slight alteration to my plumbing, I live life to the fullest. Rarely a week passes that I am not contacted to visit someone who is battling cancer. I go to be an encouragement, born of an experience that was forged on the anvil of adversity. Many times, people just need to see a survivor—someone who has overcome the very battle they are facing. Spiritually, isn't that what Christians are—survivors? Heaven is and will be filled with overcomers. The world needs to see survivors and overcomers because it gives them hope for their situation.

I had the greatest doctors and nurses that anyone could possibly hope for, and I am certain they played a role in my recovery, but I have no doubt that God Almighty played a far greater role in my survival. I was never more assured of this fact when I visited the oncologist's office four years after my chemo treatments. There were twenty-four people in the chemo study group I had participated in, and I had gotten to know several of them personally.

During the doctor's visit, I asked Dr. Bruce Roth, the oncologist who had supervised our group, how the others were doing. Looking me squarely in the eye, Dr. Roth informed me that I was the only survivor of the twenty-four. I cannot put into words the absolute sense of humility and absolute awe that overcame me.

Every day, I stand humbly in the presence of God, thanking Him for this second chance at life. I do not understand all the whys and wherefores, but I do know that God has delivered me for a purpose, and I want to spend the rest of my days fulfilling it.

I now travel extensively, particularly in Cuba, where I host pastors' conferences. Haiti, El Salvador and Ghana, West Africa, are some of the places where I have strengthened pastors and preached the gospel recently. There *is* life after cancer.

After five years of extensive checkups and tests, I no longer have to see my oncologist and have been given a clean bill of health. My cancer experience now seems like it is a million miles removed. May Jesus Christ be glorified for the marvelous things He has done in my life.

Epilogue

Joyce Meyer testifies, "My mess has become my message, and my misery has become my ministry." The same is true for me. I know things that only a survivor knows. But, to a degree, aren't we all survivors? I survived cancer, but maybe you have survived child abuse or the death of a spouse or a devastating divorce. Survivors and overcomers have a wealth of information to share with others. All of us minister most effectively through the things we have experienced. Our God does not waste our adversity.

Now there is rarely a day that goes by that I do not deal with someone who has cancer. Cancer wards and chemo units are now places where I do some of my most effective ministry. I know what cancer patients think and fret about—because I have been there. The best provision I can give them is the revelation of a survivor. They will listen to a survivor.

My mess has truly become my message. Should it not be the same for anyone who has survived the enemy's attack? Your own survival story can become a lifeline thrown out to those drowning in the whirlpool you have survived. I believe God is raising up an army of survivors who will proclaim the goodness, mercy and power of Jesus Christ. I believe He wants to put on display the magnificence of the work He has done in the lives of people who have overcome that which the devil meant for destruction. I intend to be one of those whose life is a constant source of encouragement to those who need to hear what God has done for me. I pray that you will do the same.